C000261794

ONE OF YOU IS A DEVIL

Dag Heward-Mills

Parchment House

Unless otherwise stated, all Scripture quotations are taken from the King James Version of the Bible.

Excerpts from:
Lumpkin, Joseph, B. (2010) *The Encyclopedia of Lost and Rejected Scriptures: The Pseudepigrapha and Apocrypha* 1 ed. Blountsville, Ala.: Fifth Estate. Used by permission.

ONE OF YOU IS A DEVIL

Copyright © 2017 Dag Heward-Mills

First published 2017 by Parchment House
3rd Printing 2019

[77]Find out more about Dag Heward-Mills at:

Healing Jesus Campaign
Email: evangelist@daghewardmills.org
Website: www.daghewardmills.org
Facebook: Dag Heward-Mills
Twitter: @EvangelistDag

ISBN : 978-1-68398-191-6

All rights reserved under international copyright law.
Written permission must be secured from the publisher to use or reproduce any part of this book

Contents

CHAPTER 1

How the Sins of Devils Can Become the Sins of Humans

Jesus answered them, Have not I chosen you twelve, and ONE OF YOU IS A DEVIL?

John 6:70

Jesus said to His disciples, "One of you is a devil." Jesus knew the devil from the time of his fall. He knew his depravity, his wickedness, his nature, his sins and his fall. For Jesus to say about his disciples that "One of you is a devil", was a mighty statement indeed.

It meant that one of the disciples was walking in the sins and footsteps of the devil himself. One of his disciples was behaving just like the devil. It was so easy for Jesus to recognise the devil because he knew the past glory, the sins and the downfall of Lucifer!

Today, many human beings are walking in the sins and the footsteps of Lucifer. They commit each and every single sin that Satan committed. Many pastors walk in the same steps that Lucifer walked in and end up in the same confused state of darkness that Satan is in today. Are you behaving like the devil? Are you a devil? Do you know someone who is behaving like the devil and committing all the sins that Lucifer committed?

Today, Satan is bound and restricted in chains of darkness instead of being free and happy in the realms of light and eternity. His life, his ministry and his future are destroyed because of the mistakes and sins that he made while he was an angel in heaven. He misled thousands of angels and has caused all the confusion, commotion and wickedness that is in the world today.

Many ministers live in confusion and are restricted to failure, poverty and extreme darkness. They do not even know what is happening to them. They do not understand why their ministries are so limited, restricted and poor. You are about to discover each and every one of Satan's sins and you will not walk in them after reading this book!

In this book, I want to share how you can avoid becoming a devil and dodge walking in the sins of Satan. Every minister of the gospel must earnestly desire to avoid walking in the footsteps of Lucifer who was once one of God's highest ministers. If Lucifer, who dwelt in light, could fall and cause so much confusion, how much more we who live in this dark and blind world!

CHAPTER 2

Are there Human Devils?

Jesus answered them, Have not I chosen you twelve, and ONE OF YOU IS A DEVIL?

John 6:70

You must accept that a person in your life can for a moment be a tangible living devil in action. Such a person, must not be obeyed, must not be yielded to and must not be listened to.

You must not operate by what you see. You must operate by the divine revelation of the person you are dealing with.

Certain people must be treated as devils because they are (if only for a period) literal devils to you. Some people are completely possessed and occupied by the devil! Failure to treat certain people as devils will result in serious problems. Why would I say something like that? The scripture teaches that we wrestle not against flesh and blood, but against principalities and powers. From this scripture, it is clear that our enemy is not flesh and blood but a spirit! Indeed, our wrestling, struggling and fighting is not with flesh and blood. It is with evil spirits.

However, these evil spirits are able to inhabit, influence and possess some human beings so much that it is difficult to differentiate between the human being and the devil. When this happens, human beings become literal devils and must be treated as such.

I wish to emphasize that if a human being is fully inhabited, influenced and used by the devil, you must not allow that person to function around you. I have seen ministries that were destroyed because pastors were too polite, too gentle and too restrained in their dealings with the devil. I have also seen ministries that were destroyed because pastors were too polite, too gentle and too restrained in their dealings with *people* who operated as the devil himself!

There are some human beings you must see as the devil himself. You must talk to such people as though you were talking to the devil himself! Failure to do this is to allow the devil to freely exist and manoeuvre around you and against you.

Diabolos

The word, '*diabolos*' is usually translated into the word 'devil' and refers to the literal devil. The word *diabolos* is used thirty-eight times in the entire New Testament. Thirty-five times, the word *diabolos* is translated into the word devil. For instance, "And Jesus was led into the wilderness to be tempted of the devil."

However, on three other very significant occasions, the word *diabolos* is used to describe human beings. Is that not amazing? The word *diabolos* is used to refer to none other than *Judas Iscariot,* some *pastors' wives* and some *older women.* (Please verify this for yourself). If what I am saying is in the Bible, you must believe it.

Follow the Example of Jesus Christ and Treat Certain People as Devils

1.   Jesus dealt with Peter as though he was the devil.

Peter took Him aside and began to rebuke Him, saying, " God forbid it, Lord! This shall never happen to You!"

But He turned and said to Peter, "GET BEHIND ME, SATAN! You are a stumbling block to Me; for you are not setting your mind on God's interests, but man's.

Matthew 16:22-23 (NASB)

Just like Jesus, you must accept the reality that some people are momentarily possessed and used by the devil in such a way that they become literal, tangible devils in your life. Peter, whom Jesus appointed as the leader of the church, for a moment operated as a literal devil and Jesus dealt with him sharply and conclusively. Jesus did not allow him to continue speaking in His presence. Jesus did not allow him to continue operating in His life.

Jesus Christ did not say that Peter was being *influenced* by Satan! Jesus addressed Peter as Satan himself!

Peter was familiar with Jesus. His appointment as the head of the church had perhaps gotten to his head and he had moved out of his proper place. He attempted to direct Jesus in His ministry. He began to rebuke the Son of God. He was telling Jesus to forget about the nonsense of the cross! Remember that the preaching of the cross is foolishness to many people! It was indeed foolishness to Peter on that day. He told Jesus that there was no need to carry on and go to any cross. Jesus saw through the immaturity and familiarity of Peter. But he did not say that Peter was being immature or familiar. He recognized Satan using Peter's voice. He rebuked Peter instantly and stopped Satan directly.

If people had recognized Satan's voice when Adolf Hitler was giving speeches in 1933, they would have stopped him in his tracks. But even pastors hailed this mass murderer as a hero. Adolf Hitler caused the deaths of fifty million people. He knowingly sent many people to their deaths. His last instructions were to wipe out his own German people. He said they did not deserve to live because they had lost the war. Allowing this man to speak, to live, to operate, to flourish and to become a leader was the greatest mistake that Germany ever made. Satan must be recognised and stopped in his tracks!

Do not allow the devil to operate in your life for even one minute. Be smart and fast like Jesus Christ. If you found a gaboon viper in your living room, would you allow it to stay on for a few more weeks?

Watch out for people who allow gaboon vipers to live in their living room! They are making a terrible mistake!

Watch out for people who become familiar with you!

Watch out for people who move out of place! Such people lose sight of the fact that it is not *their* place to guide, control or correct God's servant.

Dealing with the humanity of men of God may confuse you and tempt you to step out of order.

2. Jesus dealt with Judas as though he was the devil.

Jesus answered them, Have not I chosen you twelve, and ONE OF YOU IS A DEVIL?

John 6:70

Disciples and associates can turn into *diabolos* (a devil) and behave just like the devil.

Jesus called his own trusted accountant a *diabolos*. Judas Iscariot is referred to as a diabolos. Allowing a disloyal traitor to function around you can only be likened to allowing a real cobra to live and to roam freely in your house.

Do not allow any kind of disloyal person to be near you. Do not allow cobras to exist among your pastoral staff. Identify them and deal with them swiftly.

Jesus referred to Judas as a devil. He did not say that Judas was being influenced by the devil. He said Judas *was* a devil. He said "Have I not chosen you, and *one of you is a devil*." If you allow a devil to operate freely in your life and ministry, surely, you are going to have problems. Allowing a disloyal associate to operate freely in the church is the same as allowing a devil to do what he wants in the church.

Can you imagine having a rattlesnake in the living room of your house? Would you just allow it to continue to live there? Would you not treat it as a killer? If you found a black mamba in your house, would you just leave it alone? Wouldn't you treat it as something very dangerous to your life? Would you not treat it as something that brings death? Would you not do everything to get it out of your life? Would you not try to kill it? I believe a snake must be treated as a source of death and not like a pet. A venomous snake is not a pet! A venomous snake does not deserve any kindness and it knows that it will not receive any kindness from you. That is why snakes hide all the time!

Jesus Christ considered disloyal Judas as someone very dangerous. He called him a devil! This is how you must deal with disloyal people who turn against you and betray you. All pastors who have a light-hearted attitude towards disloyalty live to regret it.

If Jesus Christ dealt with somebody as a devil why do you consider yourself to be wiser? It is your great mistake to deal with disloyalty as though it were something trivial. Your church cannot grow because you have allowed a cobra to roam around freely. You are treating the "cobra assistant" as a pet instead of treating him as a dangerous enemy! You are treating your "black mamba associate" as a pet instead of treating him as a source of death and destruction!

3. **Jesus dealt with the Pharisees as though they were devils.**

Ye serpents, ye GENERATION OF VIPERS, how can ye escape the damnation of hell?

Matthew 23:33

Pray for the spirit of discernment so that you will be like Jesus. It takes great discernment to see evil in religious people. It takes great discernment to see through the righteous façade that religious people present. Indeed, few of us have real discernment and so we call bad things good and good things bad.

Woe unto them that call evil good, and good evil; that put darkness for light, and light for darkness; that put bitter for sweet, and sweet for bitter!

Isaiah 5:20

Jesus spoke to the Pharisees and described them as a generation of snakes. He addressed them as vipers. They were spiritual vipers – poisonous, deadly and evil. Jesus also told the Pharisees that they were just like their father the devil. If the father is a devil, it stands to reason that the son is also a devil!

Ye are of YOUR FATHER THE DEVIL, and the lusts of YOUR FATHER ye will do. He was a MURDERER **from the beginning, and abode not in the truth, because there is no truth in him.** When he speaketh a lie, he **speaketh of his own: for he is a liar, and the father of it.**

John 8:44

It is important to deal with those who oppose the anointing and kill the ministry of the man of God. It was these Pharisees who eventually murdered Jesus Christ on the cross. But Jesus knew all along that they were devils and murderers. That is why Jesus called these pastors vipers. Jesus Christ confronted them and dealt with them as what they really were – devils! Long before they murdered Jesus Christ, Jesus called them devils and dealt with them as such.

4. Paul warned pastors' wives not to be devils.

Even so must their wives be grave, not slanderers (DIABOLOS), sober, faithful in all things.

1 Timothy 3:11

Can you believe that Apostle Paul used the word "*diabolos*" (devil) to describe some pastors' wives and deacons' wives? The translators of the Bible translated the word "*diabolos*" as devil in other parts of the Bible but did not translate it as devil in this scripture. Perhaps the translators were scared to apply the word "devil" to the pastors' wives. Most of the translators were pastors and would be hesitant to write such things. But the Word is the Word! And the truth is the truth! Pastors' wives and deacons' wives can turn into devils. "*Diabolos*" is the Greek word for devil. That is why Paul warned pastors' wives not to turn into devils. Deacons' wives are warned not to turn into *diabolos*.

Why would Paul warn pastors' wives not to turn into devils? It is because a pastor's wife can become a strong accuser and opposer of her husband. A pastor's wife can also become a strong challenger to her husband. Through accusation and opposition, some women are transformed into literal human devils that their husbands have to contend with.

Not all pastors have good marriages! Some have good marriages. Some have average marriages and some have terrible marriages. Adoniram Judson was called "three times lucky" because he married three times and each marriage was a good one. William Carey married three times. He had one bad marriage and two good marriages.

There are many men of God who are dealing with tangible, physical female devils in their homes. Some of them would tell you that the greatest opposition and challenge to their lives and ministry is the woman they are married to. Why is this? Unfortunately, many beautiful ladies quickly metamorphose into full time accusers, opposers and challengers of the man of God they married. These pastors have to deal with a literal tangible, physical devil at home.

5.   **Paul warned older women not to be devils.**

> **But speak thou the things which become sound doctrine: that the aged men be sober, grave, temperate, sound in faith, in charity, in patience.**
>
> **The aged women likewise, that they be in behaviour as becometh holiness, not false accusers (DIABOLOS), not given to much wine, teachers of good things;**
>
> **Titus 2:1-3**

Older women are also susceptible to turning into devils. Older women can turn into *diabolos* and behave just like the devil. I did not write the Bible. Neither do I want to re-write it. Let's read it together and accept what we see. The scripture clearly means that older women can become false accusers, slanderers, opposers, challengers and devils! That is what *diabolos* means. Why is that? Many older women are disappointed, disillusioned and disheartened about life. The disappointments of life have a way of turning people away from joy, peace, cheerfulness and love.

Many women (and men) never experience what they hoped for. Many have had their expectations dashed. This deep disappointment with life, opens the door to devils. Some older, often bitter, women become inhabited by devils. The cheerfulness, giggles, smiles and friendliness of the young sweet girl are replaced by bitterness, wickedness, jealousy, hatred, irritation and unpleasantness. An older woman can literally become a devil. Keep your eyes open, you will see it practically. This could be why some older men go looking for younger, more cheerful, happier, loving girls whose souls are not embittered and open to demonic oppression.

CHAPTER 3

The Past Glory of Lucifer

Son of man, take up a lamentation upon the king of Tyrus, and say unto him, Thus saith the Lord God; Thou sealest up the sum, full of wisdom, and perfect in beauty. THOU HAST BEEN IN EDEN THE GARDEN OF GOD; every precious stone was thy covering, the sardius, topaz, and the diamond, the beryl, the onyx, and the jasper, the sapphire, the emerald, and the carbuncle, and gold: the workmanship of thy tabrets and of thy pipes was prepared in thee in the day that thou wast created. Thou art the anointed cherub that covereth; and I have set thee so: THOU WAST UPON THE HOLY MOUNTAIN OF GOD; thou hast walked up and down in the midst of the stones of fire. Thou wast perfect in thy ways from the day that thou wast created, till iniquity was found in thee.

Ezekiel 28:12-15

S atan used to be a good person and a good angel in heaven. Satan was called Lucifer when he was a good angel. Perhaps, you were not even as good as Satan was in his "good" days. Many people are given good things by God, set up by God, and anointed in His presence.

You may be a good person today. However if Satan fell from his glorious position, so can you. It is important to remain humble. It is important to distance yourself from any traits of separatism, independence, rebellion against authority and disobedience. These sinful tendencies turned a perfect angel into a monstrous and wicked creature.

Satan has been transformed into an unrecognizable monster! He has fallen from his shiny, attractive and perfect state! It is important to know how good the devil was so that you know the extent to which a person can be transformed by sin.

All of us worship leaders, singers, pastors, and associate pastors must take note of who Lucifer really was. He was greater and nicer than most of us. Yet, he changed so much when evil entered into him. Many churches have associate pastors who are the nicest and the best. They are the most anointed and the most likely to take over from their leaders when the time comes. This is exactly how Lucifer was. Lucifer was once anointed, charming and admired by all. When sin entered into him, he changed so much and broke the hearts of all who loved him. God had no other choice than to throw him out of heaven. Similarly, many senior pastors have no other choice than to throw their senior associates out of the church when treachery enters their hearts.

1. **Satan was once a cherub, which is a kind of angel.** Many associates, singers, worship leaders, pastors are angelic in their presentation to the congregation.

Thou art THE ANOINTED CHERUB that covereth; and I have set thee so: thou wast upon the holy mountain of

God; thou hast walked up and down in the midst of the stones of fire.

Ezekiel 28:14

2. **Satan was once an anointed and elevated angel, appointed by God.** Many associates, singers, worship leaders, and pastors are elevated, anointed and appointed before the congregation.

Thou art the anointed cherub that covereth; AND I HAVE SET THEE SO: thou wast upon the holy mountain of God; thou hast walked up and down in the midst of the stones of fire.

Ezekiel 28:14

3. **Satan was once in the Garden of Eden.** Many associates, singers, worship leaders, and pastors have been in the church for many years. They have had many experiences and can tell you what it was like to be in "Eden".

THOU HAST BEEN IN EDEN the garden of God;…

Ezekiel 28:13

4. **Satan was one of the archangels who was present when God created the earth.** Many associates, singers, worship leaders, and pastors were there from the very beginning of the church. They saw the rise of the church. They saw the pastor grow and become a "man of God". It is because these people were there from the beginning that they think that they are as good as the leader. Perhaps Lucifer thought he was God because he was present when God laid the foundations of the earth.

WHERE WAST THOU WHEN I LAID THE FOUNDATIONS OF THE EARTH? Declare, if thou hast understanding.

Who hath laid the measures thereof, if thou knowest? Or who hath stretched the line upon it?

Whereupon are the foundations thereof fastened? Or who laid the corner stone thereof; when the morning stars sang together, AND ALL THE SONS OF GOD SHOUTED FOR JOY?

Job 38:4-7

5. **Satan was once musically gifted. The musical gift is a special gift.** People love music! People praise musicians and singers! Lucifer stood in this musical office. Whenever people praise and admire you, you forget that you are nothing in actual fact. I recently met a famous worship leader who was deceived into thinking he was something that he was not. When he was thrown off the platform that made him famous, he became a withered branch and could do nothing for himself. O, how sad it is for me to watch gifted musicians and singers amount to nothing because of deception. Many musically gifted people have turned into withered branches just like Lucifer. The story of Lucifer has been repeated again and again in the lives of Christian musicians.

Thou hast been in Eden the garden of God; every precious stone was thy covering, the sardius, topaz, and the diamond, the beryl, the onyx, and the jasper, the sapphire, the emerald, and the carbuncle, and gold: the workmanship of THY TABRETS AND OF THY PIPES WAS PREPARED IN THEE in the day that thou wast created.

Thou art the anointed cherub that covereth; and I have set thee so: thou wast upon the holy mountain of God; thou hast walked up and down in the midst of the stones of fire.

Thou wast perfect in thy ways from the day that thou wast created, till iniquity was found in thee.

Ezekiel 28:13-15

6. **Satan once walked in the corridors of fire and power.** Many associates, singers, worship leaders, and pastors have walked in power and authority.

Thou art the anointed cherub that covereth; and I have set thee so: thou wast upon THE HOLY MOUNTAIN OF GOD; THOU HAST WALKED UP AND DOWN IN THE MIDST OF THE STONES OF FIRE.

Ezekiel 28:14

7. **Satan was once anointed.** Many associates, singers, worship leaders, and pastors are genuinely anointed by God. Most of my associates, pastors and musicians are genuinely anointed.

Thou art THE ANOINTED CHERUB THAT COVERETH; AND I HAVE SET THEE SO: thou wast upon the holy mountain of God; thou hast walked up and down in the midst of the stones of fire.

Ezekiel 28:14

8. **Satan was once beautiful and attractive.** Many associates, singers, worship leaders, and pastors are attractive. You will find the congregation being drawn to them. You will find the congregation liking them and talking to them often. Associates, assistants and pastors will easily recognise that they are liked. It is this natural attraction that feeds a deception that you are what you are not!

Thine heart was lifted up because of THY BEAUTY, thou hast corrupted thy wisdom by reason of thy brightness: I will cast thee to the ground, I will lay thee before kings, that they may behold thee.

Ezekiel 28:17

9. **Satan was once a bright and shining person.** Many associates, singers, worship leaders, pastors are shining stars. They can see themselves shine on the stage. They

attract attention and enjoy the limelight. But the limelight can be dangerous for those who are not schooled in humility and reality.

Thine heart was lifted up because of thy beauty, thou hast corrupted thy wisdom by reason of THY BRIGHTNESS: I will cast thee to the ground, I will lay thee before kings, that they may behold thee.

Ezekiel 28:17

10. **Satan was once called a son.** Many associates, singers, worship leaders, and pastors are true sons of the ministry. This is why the disloyalty and breaking away of associates, singers, and worship leaders causes so much heartbreak in the church.

How art thou fallen from heaven, O LUCIFER, SON OF THE MORNING! ...

Isaiah 14:12

11. **Satan was once perfect. Many associates, singers, worship leaders, and pastors are perfect gentlemen.** Many associates, singers, worship leaders, and pastors are perfect ministers of the gospel. Many associates, singers, worship leaders, and pastors are perfect husbands.

Thou WAST PERFECT in thy ways from the day that thou wast created, till iniquity was found in thee.

Ezekiel 28:15

CHAPTER 4

The Sins and Fall
of Lucifer

And God saw every thing that he had made, and,
behold, it was very good. …

Genesis 1:31

God created good things! God saw everything that He had made and knew that it was good! So how did a wicked and cruel creature like Satan come into existence? Where did all the evil in our world arise from? Where are all the dreadful murders, tortures and sad events in our world from? Where are all the monsters in our world from? Where are all the demons and evil spirits in our world from? What inspires men to do so much evil?

Well, there are clear points that led to the existence of Satan as we know him today. The Bible gives us glimpses into the creation of the evil world. There are seven clear steps that have led to the existence of fallen angels. God did not set about to create evil. God saw all that He had created and knew that it was good. God created good things! God created very good things! Somehow, evil also came into existence. Let's now go through the steps that led to the existence of Satan.

1. The creation of free-willed angels:

Angels are good spirits that were created by the Lord. The Bible clearly teaches us that angels were made by God in heaven. "For by him were all things created, that are in heaven, and that are in earth, visible and invisible, whether *they be* thrones, or dominions, or principalities, or powers: all things were created by him, and for him:" (Colossians 1:16). A special but important quality that angels possess, is their free will. This free will is the important quality that would allow angels to obey or disobey God if they wanted to. Most of us think that angels do not have a choice as to whether they want to serve God or not. But they do! God gave them a free will. And that is why some of them were able to rebel.

2. The creation of archangels:

The second step leading to the existence of evil spirits is the establishment of superior angels in the angel community. The Bible makes mention of three of these archangels or senior angels.

Michael is specifically referred to as an archangel.

"Yet Michael the archangel, when contending with the devil he disputed about the body of Moses, durst not bring against him a railing accusation, but said, The Lord rebuke thee" (Jude 1:9).

Michael is also referred to as a chief prince.

"But the prince of the kingdom of Persia withstood me one and twenty days: but, lo, Michael, one of the chief princes, came to help me; and I remained there with the kings of Persia" (Daniel 10:13).

Another prominent angel who is mentioned is angel Gabriel, who was sent to Mary to announce the birth of Jesus and also sent to Zachariah to announce the birth of John the Baptist.

And in the sixth month the angel Gabriel was sent from God unto a city of Galilee, named Nazareth, To a virgin espoused to a man whose name was Joseph, of the house of David; and the virgin's name was Mary.

Luke 1:26-27

And there appeared unto him an angel of the Lord standing on the right side of the altar of incense. And when Zacharias saw him, he was troubled, and fear fell upon him. But the angel said unto him, Fear not, Zacharias: for thy prayer is heard; and thy wife Elisabeth shall bear thee a son, and thou shalt call his name John . . .

And Zacharias said unto the angel, Whereby shall I know this? for I am an old man, and my wife well stricken in years. And the angel answering said unto him, I am Gabriel, that stand in the presence of God; and am sent to speak unto thee, and to shew thee these glad tidings

Luke 1:11-13, 18-19

The other prominent angel mentioned in the Bible is Lucifer. When he was a good angel, he was called the "anointed cherub" who walked up and down in the holy mountain of God.

Thou art the anointed cherub that covereth; and I have set thee so: thou wast upon the holy mountain of God; thou hast walked up and down in the midst of the stones of fire.

Ezekiel 28:14

These passages give us the impression that there were only three archangels but there are probably several other archangels.

As you know, the Bible mentions "a host of angels" and "thousands of angels". There are millions of angels around us. Indeed, other manuscripts like the Book of Enoch describe other senior angels and even give them names like Raphael, Uriel, Raguel, Ramiel and Sariel. Remember that Michael the archangel was only one of several chief princes.

3. The pride, independence and separatism of an archangel.

The third step leading up to the existence of Satan and evil spirits is the development of pride and independence in one of the senior/arch angels.

The evil of *separatism, independence and pride* entered the heart of one of the senior angels who had been created in purity and innocence.

Notice how an independent vision developed in Lucifer's heart when he said, "I will ascend! I will be like the Most High!"

"How art thou fallen from heaven, O Lucifer, son of the morning! How art thou cut down to the ground, which didst weaken the nations! For thou hast said in thine heart, *I will ascend* into heaven, *I will exalt* my throne above the stars of God: *I will sit* also upon the mount of the congregation, in the sides of the north: *I will ascend* above the heights of the clouds; *I will be like* the most High. Yet thou shalt be brought down to hell, to the sides of the pit" (Isaiah 14:12-15).

Satan's speech was full of "I will", "I will be", "I will exalt", "I will ascend". It was not "We will", "We will be", "We will rise". He had developed an independent and separate agenda. He wanted to get somewhere and he wanted to become something independently. He felt he did not need God. He felt independent. He did not want God. He felt like being on his own. He wanted to be like God! In fact, he wanted to displace God if possible.

Be careful about trying to be separate and independent! It is a satanic trait and it is what has brought all the evil that we have in our world today. Try to stay together! Fight the tendency to be separate! Fight the tendency to be alone! The desire to separate originates from Lucifer.

Watch out when you experience the urge to separate yourself from your fellowship and family.

4.   The rejection of the independent archangel by loyal angels.

Apparently, this independent, prideful and separatist attitude by the senior archangel was not received well by many other angels. Most of the angels rejected Lucifer's ideas to separate and become independent. Several angels were offended by Lucifer's prideful ideas. Some angels however, were deceived and actually thought that Lucifer's ideas to separate and be independent would work.

Throughout the Bible, you find various conflicts erupting between good angels and bad angels. The independent, disloyal, prideful and separatist angels were rejected by other loyal angels. The loyal angels were not impressed with the separatist ideas and had no intention of following them. This brought about a conflict between good angels and bad angels. There was now a war in the family of angels. Angels who had been brothers and family friends for thousands of years were forced to become enemies of each other.

Peaceful heaven was transformed into a place of conflict. Angels disagreed on the independent archangel's ideas to be separate. Angels engaged in fights at their level without any interference from God Himself. God seems to have allowed them to fight it out. God expects you to fight for what is right and not just sit back allow evil and separatism to flourish.

Some angels fought for the honour of God, whilst the independent, wicked, pride-filled, discontented and disloyal angels fought to carve out for themselves a separate existence.

Every church has people who seek a separate and independent agenda. These are the separatists who follow the Satanic pattern. God expects the good angels and the loyal people to fearlessly fight the separatists.

Do not be bewildered because you have to fight disloyal people. You will always have to fight disloyal people. Do not be sad when you have to fight your own brothers because of the honour of God. It is a choice you have to make. Michael, Lucifer and Gabriel were good friends and brothers before the rebellion. It is a sad thing to have to fight your own brother. Michael and Gabriel had to make the choice to part with their long-standing friend and brother, Lucifer.

Thankfully, Michael and Gabriel chose to oppose their brother, Lucifer. I do not think it was easy for Gabriel and Michael to make that decision. But they chose right! They chose to support the higher authority! They rejected Lucifer's ideas! They pointed out to him that he was making a mistake. They told Lucifer to repent and to stop speaking those high-sounding and prideful words. Lucifer must have been surprised at Gabriel's attitude! Perhaps, he thought that the more junior archangel would be sympathetic to his vision. Perhaps Lucifer thought Gabriel would follow his leadership as the anointed cherub who walked up and down the holy mountain on the coals of fire.

Gabriel, however, was not fooled. Michael was adamant that Lucifer had gone mad. Michael and Gabriel probably had several meetings with Lucifer to resolve the crisis. They probably shared God's wisdom with Lucifer, but he was too proud to listen to them.

Lucifer probably told Gabriel and Michael, "You guys don't know much. I have been here from the beginning. I've been through a lot. I've been up and down that holy mountain for a thousand years. There is no future here! You can never be promoted here! You can never rise up above those who were here before you! Only one person is promoted in this system!"

It is these kinds of words that birthed the first break-up and rebellion. It is these kinds of words that spoil churches. It is this kind of speaking that breeds confusion in the church. It is this separatist attitude that Satan seeks to impart to men, making them independent, conflict-prone and separatist. It is this negative and independent attitude of Lucifer that brought all the conflict, quarrel and division into peaceful heaven.

It is good that Michael would not stand for Lucifer's nonsense. Loyal assistants must not tolerate this kind of rubbish. Do not let rebellious people destroy the honour of God. Do not let disloyal people break up the church.

Fighting disloyal people is a good thing! Never retreat from a good fight against the evil of disloyalty. It is a good and angelic trait to fight against people who want to destroy the peace and divide the family and the church. Fight disloyalty with all your heart. Do not step back from the open confrontation with evil. Jesus is building His church! You must fight all those who are breaking it down! Don't try to be nicer or better than the good angels of heaven!

Indeed, there are several well-documented fights between good angels and bad separatist angels.

The Bible records an all-out war between loyal angels and independent rebellious angels. This all-out war was between Michael, the angels under his command, and the dragon and his angels. (Angelic Battle 1)

And there was war in heaven: Michael and his angels fought against the dragon; and the dragon fought and his angels,

Revelation 12:7

There is another recorded fight between Michael and a being called the prince of Persia. (Angelic Battle 2)

> **But the prince of the kingdom of Persia withstood me one and twenty days: but, lo, Michael, one of the chief princes, came to help me; and I remained there with the kings of Persia.**
>
> **Daniel 10:13**

There is also a recorded confrontation between Michael and Satan over the body of Moses. (Angelic Battle 3)

> **Yet Michael the archangel, when contending with the devil he disputed about the body of Moses, durst not bring against him a railing accusation, but said, The Lord rebuke thee.**
>
> **Jude 1:9**

5. **The defeat and casting away of the independent and rebellious angels by loyal angels.**

The Bible records the defeat of the dragon and his angels by the good angels.

"And the great dragon was cast out, that old serpent, called the Devil, and Satan, which deceiveth the whole world: he was cast out into the earth, and his angels were cast out with him." (Revelation 12:9).

After the good angels successfully routed Lucifer and his followers, it was clear that they would not be welcome in heaven any longer. The bad angels were so bad that they would have to be dismissed! Indeed, the doors and windows of heaven were opened and Lucifer was thrown down to the earth.

People who develop an independent spirit and a separatist attitude lose their position and place in the church. These angels suffered terribly for the mistake of trying to separate themselves from God. Instead of trying to separate yourself, find out how to get closer and stay connected to God and to His church. Always remember the scripture in Jude 19 "These be they who separate themselves, sensual, having not the Spirit."

Satan wants to separate you. Make sure he is not successful in turning you into one of the separatist and fallen angels. Do not allow yourself to follow the twisted minds of discontented and rebellious pastors!

6. The transformation of Lucifer: From an anointed cherub into a dragon.

Upon the fall of Lucifer, his outward nature was transformed into an ugly dragon. A terrible degenerative darkness and ugliness came upon him and he became a dragon. We know that this ugly dragon was originally a beautiful angel because the Bible says so. It is amazing how sin can turn a beautiful person into the ugliest and darkest creature. "And the great dragon was cast out, that old serpent, called the Devil, and Satan, which deceiveth the whole world: he was cast out into the earth, and his angels were cast out with him" (Revelation 12:9).

Satan is now this contorted and twisted creature without a home nor a resting place who is forced to roam around on earth, far below his original glorious position. You should see the fallen state of some associate pastors who moved out of their position. Their ill-fated lives can only be described as dark, distorted and unfortunate.

Satan's banishment to the earth was a step towards his permanent locking up in hell. Many criminals are taken from prison to prison, while they serve their sentence. Lucifer is equally moving from prison to prison as he serves his sentence for rebellion.

7. The wandering of the displaced dragon and fallen angels on earth.

With the banishment from heaven, the dragon and his angels became homeless, banished beings who roam about on the earth. It is these beings with their leader who are today known as Satan and the princes of the underworld. In the book of Daniel, the evil powers that fought Michael were called princes. They are princes because they were probably powerful or senior angels before they fell. As we said earlier, there are thousands and thousands of angels. Unfortunately, the rebellion misled a section of the angels of both junior and senior ranks.

"But the prince of the kingdom of Persia withstood me one and twenty days: but, lo, Michael, one of the chief princes, came to help me; and I remained there with the kings of Persia" (Daniel 10:13).

In the New Testament, we are told that the princes of this world wanted to crucify Jesus Christ and actually followed through with their plan to do so. The princes of this world are the fallen archangels and senior angels who wield authority over evil spirits in the dark world.

"Howbeit we speak wisdom among them that are perfect: yet not the wisdom of this world, nor of the princes of this world, that come to nought: But we speak the wisdom of God in a mystery, *even* the hidden *wisdom*, which God ordained before the world unto our glory: Which none of the princes of this world knew: for had they known *it*, they would not have crucified the Lord of glory" (1 Corinthians 2:6-8).

Jesus Christ has been raised up above all such fallen angels and authorities. He has been given power and dominion over all wicked creatures, wherever they may be.

Which he wrought in Christ, when he raised him from the dead, and set him at his own right hand in the heavenly places,

Far above all principality, and power, and might, and dominion, and every name that is named, not only in this world, but also in that which is to come:

Ephesians 1:20-21

CHAPTER 5

The Sins and Fall of Lucifer's Princes

And there was war in heaven: Michael and his angels fought against the dragon; and THE DRAGON FOUGHT AND HIS ANGELS, And prevailed not; neither was their place found any more in heaven. And the great dragon was cast out, that old serpent, called the Devil, and Satan, which deceiveth the whole world: he was cast out into the earth, and HIS ANGELS WERE CAST OUT WITH HIM.

Revelation 12:7-9

I t is obvious, from numerous references in the Bible that apart from Satan, there are other creatures which exist in the invisible world. These creatures are important to us because they are equally evil and are mentioned as opposing us, fighting us and causing problems for human beings.

Jesus Christ came into the world to defeat and destroy the devil and his fallen angels.

The term "Satan" refers to diabolos and the devil, that old serpent who deceived Adam and Eve and entered into the world of human beings.

The term "princes of this world" refers to the fallen angels who followed the devil in his rebellion and were thrown down from heaven.

Steps to the Creation of the Fallen Princes of This World

1. **Lucifer is created and placed in heaven as a senior and superior angel.** His superior status is given to him by God. The scripture is very clear on this.

   You were the anointed cherub who covers, And I PLACED YOU THERE. You were on the holy mountain of God; you walked in the midst of the stones of fire. You were blameless in your ways from the day YOU WERE CREATED, until unrighteousness was found in you.

   Ezekiel 28:14-15, NASB.

2. **Lucifer is created with a free will and has to choose to serve God or to rebel.** Lucifer chose to be a rebel and became a fallen archangel.

   Ye are of your father the devil, and the lusts of your father ye will do. He was a murderer from the beginning,

and ABODE NOT IN THE TRUTH, because there is no truth in him. When he speaketh a lie, he speaketh of his own: for he is a liar, and the father of it.

John 8:44

Lucifer did not continue to live in truth. He abode not in truth. He had a choice to abide in truth or to walk away from the truth. He chose not to abide in truth. He was so full of self-deception and is today the father of all deception. Lucifer believed that he could successfully rebel against God Himself. He believed in this lie so much that he actually launched out against his creator.

3. **Several other angels became fallen angels:** This happened after Lucifer inspired other angels to rebel against their creator. The other angels were deceived into rising up in rebellion alongside Lucifer.

Some senior angels also believed the lie and followed Satan in the rebellion. This rebellion led to a group of fallen archangels and fallen ordinary angels. Satan is the father of evil and of all fallen angels. Fallen angels received their inspiration from Satan. Satan is the chief of the fallen angels and is known as the old serpent, the dragon, the accuser of the brethren and the prince of this world.

Satan has many titles because there are many evil things that he is the originator of. Today, Satan is the leader of the many fallen angels he inspired. Today, Satan is the leader of all rebellious, independent, ungrateful discontented, separatist and disloyal fallen princes.

...Satan, which deceiveth the whole world: he was cast out into the earth, *and HIS ANGELS* WERE CAST OUT WITH HIM.

Revelation 12:9

4. **Lucifer became the prince of this world by deceiving Adam and Eve to entrust themselves to him.**

The devil, *diabolos*, is also called the prince of this world. Why is he called the prince of this world? Was he created as a prince of our world? No, certainly not! Through deception and trickery, Satan entered the world of human beings! Adam and Eve believed the deception and entrusted themselves to Lucifer's leadership. Lucifer, the fallen archangel gained control over the human world because Adam and Eve followed him and became his subjects.

Now the serpent was more subtil than any beast of the field which the Lord God had made. And he said unto the woman, Yea, hath God said, Ye shall not eat of every tree of the garden.

Genesis 3:1

Satan has slowly destroyed and perverted the world of humans. The human race is now completely destroyed because of Satan's influence on mankind. The devil, *diabolos*, offered Jesus the kingdoms of this world because he is the evil prince that dominates this world.

Man has become evil, perverted and sinful. Man's ways are constantly directed towards self-destruction. "...Also, the heart of the sons of men is full of evil, and madness is in their heart while they live, and after that they go to the dead" (Ecclesiastes 9:3). This unfortunate state of human beings is caused by the prince of this world.

When God sent His son into this world to save mankind from sin and evil, Satan immediately recognised him and opposed his presence on the earth. Satan organised the wicked men on this earth to crucify a sinless, loving preacher. Jesus was crucified by religious men who were in fact, influenced by Satan. Speaking about His crucifixion, Jesus said to His disciples, "...The prince of this world cometh and hath nothing in me" (John 14:30). He also said, "...Now shall the prince of this world be cast out" (John 12:31). From the verses above, you can see that fallen angels and princes are very active in bringing about evil in the world today.

5. **Other fallen angels quickly took up positions in different parts of the world and became princes of the world.**

For we wrestle not against flesh and blood, but against PRINCIPALITIES, against powers, against the rulers of the darkness of this world, against spiritual wickedness in high places.

Ephesians 6:12

Lucifer is called the *prince* of this world and his fallen angels are called *princes* of this world. The word "prince of this world" comes from the Greek word "ARCHON" which means commander, ruler or chief leader. This is the same word that is translated "principalities". We wrestle not against flesh and blood but against "ARCHON". This means that we wrestle against commanders and rulers. Who are these commanders and rulers? Who gave them their power and what do they rule over?

These commanders are fallen senior angels associated with Lucifer. It is evident from the scripture that there is a group of commander angels who are affecting the activities in this world. Notice "Howbeit we speak wisdom among them that are perfect: yet not the wisdom of this world, nor of the PRINCES OF THIS WORLD, that come to nought" (1 Corinthians 2:6).

The prince of this world is also always associated with other princes in this world. Notice that the crucifixion of Jesus Christ is blamed on a group of entities called the "princes of this world".

"Which none of the PRINCES OF THIS WORLD knew: for had they known it, they would not have crucified the Lord of glory" (1 Corinthians 2:8).

Jesus Christ was crucified through the actions and activities of the princes of this world who are fallen archangels. Jesus Christ was killed by the princes of this world who were acting through the Pharisees.

These fallen archangels do not have all wisdom. If they did, they would not have crucified the Lord of all glory. Through the crucifixion of Jesus Christ and the shedding of His blood, the princes of this world have actually been destroyed. These archangels would have prevented the crucifixion of Christ if they knew what it meant.

CHAPTER 6

The Sins of a Devil: Conflict With Authority

For thou hast said in thine heart, I WILL ASCEND INTO HEAVEN, I will exalt my throne above the stars of God: I will sit also upon the mount of the congregation, in the sides of the north: I will ascend above the heights of the clouds; I will be like the most High.

Isaiah 14:13-14

"One of you is a devil!"

How can you know when someone is a devil?

When somebody is a devil, he behaves exactly like the devil and rises against authority just as the devil did!

Lucifer was in heaven and he had conflict with God although God never did anything to Lucifer. People who constantly have conflicts with their seniors are inspired by Satan. It is a very bad sign when people constantly have conflict with seniors, overseers and supervisors. Watch out for that sign and it will help you to know when somebody has become a devil.

Satan is the great inspirer of all who fight against authority. I remember one pastor who was transferred from church to church at different occasions of his life. Each time I thought to myself, our brother is going to bear fruit in this new location. But it was not to be so. In each location he went to, he had problems with the overseer.

He would not comply with instructions. He would not answer his calls. At meetings, he would provoke extensive discussions over little issues. He would oppose ideas that came up. He would not attend certain meetings. Surely, this pattern of conflict with authority was a bad sign. Eventually, he became a full-blown rebel and began to insult and accuse the bishops in the church. He was eventually dismissed. I thought to myself, "This fellow has been showing signs of Satan's presence in his life for many years."

Believe it or not, Satan had great conflict with God Himself. Satan even attempted to displace God from His place of authority. Satan tried to ascend into the throne of God. People who are influenced by Satan have this same characteristic; they have conflicts with those above them.

They try to ascend out of their place and challenge divinely ordained authorities. The challenging of leaders was first done by Satan and has been the practice of all his followers.

Watch out for those who constantly have problems with parents, with leadership and with authorities! Watch out for people who do not like to be told what to do! Watch out for those who cannot stand it when they are guided or counselled! Watch out for those who react angrily to correction!

Watch out for those who go into bad moods after they are told off! Watch out for those who do not like their fathers! Watch out for those who do not like their mothers! Watch out for people who insult grown-ups, senior pastors and other men of authority!

Watch out for people who can stand up to fathers and embarrass them! Watch out for those who never get along with fathers, mothers, pastors and other authorities! Watch out for those who are always having some conflict with their boss at work! Watch out for those who can shout at their mothers!

CHAPTER 7

The Sins of a Devil: Misleading Colleagues

And there was war in heaven: Michael and his angels fought against the dragon; and the dragon fought and HIS ANGELS,

And prevailed not; neither was their place found any more in heaven.

And the great dragon was cast out, that old serpent, called the Devil, and Satan, which deceiveth the whole world: he was cast out into the earth, and HIS ANGELS WERE CAST OUT WITH HIM.

Revelation 12:7-9

"One of you is a devil!"

How can you know when someone is a devil?

When somebody is a devil, he behaves exactly like the devil and misleads his colleagues just as the devil did! Lucifer misled a large number of angels to rebel against their creator. He misled senior angels who are now principalities and wicked spirits in high places.

Satan has imparted this nature to some men. These men in turn rise up and mislead associates, friends and important people to turn away from the one who appointed them and made them who they are.

Pastors who mislead fellow pastors are inspired by Satan. Lucifer, through fair speeches and convincing arguments, took fellow angels with him into darkness. That is what it means to have a devil in your church. Someone who turns the hearts of the people against the leader or the founder is a living devil!

I once had a pastor who convinced six other pastors and the entire choir to follow him to create a breakaway church. Several people left my church and the church was severely weakened. I experienced what it means to have a devil in my church. When you have a devil in the church, you have a character like Lucifer who convinces people to turn against their real leader.

On another occasion, we sent a pastor with eight families to start a branch of our church in a city of Europe. (Eight families is a large number of people for a European church). This pastor, just like Lucifer, spoke to the families whom I had entrusted to him. He explained to them that I was from Ghana and I did not care much about people from his country. (This pastor also hailed from an English-speaking West African country near Ghana). He explained to them that I had built several churches in Ghana, but not much had been done in his native country. After months of secretly convincing the important people in the church, he suddenly resigned. When he resigned, the entire congregation resigned with him and followed him to his new church. That European church was closed down by the activities of this fellow.

Remember that the devil comes to steal, to kill and to destroy. This brother came into my life and ministry to steal, to kill and to destroy the church I had started. He wiped out an entire church! That is what it is like to have a devil in the church. He will destroy everything and wipe you out.

Dear friend, it is not difficult to see that such people walk in the exact same sins of Lucifer who convinced other archangels and senior angels to follow him. Satan is the great inspirer of all breakaway and rebellious factions.

I remember one pastor who would not communicate properly. Like all those who do not communicate properly, he began to operate like a silent serpent. One day, he came up and declared his intention to separate himself from the church. Unknown to me, he had been conspiring to do this for some time. He left with a team of three other older pastors.

After they resigned, they began to make fun of me and mock my teachings on loyalty. Some of them would even play my tapes and laugh at me. They would gather around to listen to a tape where I was preaching and like a group of mocking birds, make fun of me and my messages.

However, as time went by, they experienced trouble after trouble until one of them experienced a terrible tragedy. After this tragedy, some of them came back to ask for prayer and forgiveness.

Satan inspired his colleague angels to turn against their creator. The angels were misled, and fell into darkness and destruction. These fellows who mocked me were equally devastated.

When Satan's influence spread in heaven, several of the angels were misled. Several angels believed the lies that were told them. It seems that thousands and thousands of angels were misled by the lying speeches of Lucifer. These unfortunate angels were promised important positions in the same way that Adam and Eve were promised great things. Remember that Adam and Eve were promised the status of gods.

These unfortunate angels must have been promised many things if they would join in the rebellion. Just as politicians today promise many things but are unable to do them, Satan could not give the angels any of the things he promised.

To be misled by a liar and a thief is a very painful thing indeed. Satan is the father of all lies and deceptions. Is there a dangerous opinion leader who goes around polluting the minds of important people? Have you put a Lucifer in charge of a church, a fellowship or a committee? Is there someone in your church who behaves exactly like Lucifer? You can be sure that they will turn the minds of the people against you. That is what it means to have a devil in your church! Watch out for people who turn the hearts of the loyal members away from the leader!

It is time to block the devil! It is time to call a devil a devil! It is time to fight against our enemy!

CHAPTER 8

The Sins of a Devil: Starting Quarrels and Wars

And **THERE WAS WAR IN HEAVEN:** Michael and his angels fought against the dragon; and the dragon fought and his angels

Revelation 12:7

"One of you is a devil!"

How can you know when someone is a devil?

When somebody is a devil, he behaves exactly like the devil and starts quarrels and wars just as the devil did!

Satan is the one who introduced war, confusion, quarrels, contention and strife in a place where there was peace. Heaven enjoyed peace, harmony, love and tranquillity until Satan introduced confusion! Can you imagine *war* in heaven?

The commotion caused by the rebellion of Satan was an unfortunate disturbance of the peace of heaven. It was an act of the highest disrespect to the Creator of heaven and earth. It is no wonder that Satan and his angels were simply thrown out of heaven to await a final confinement in the lake of fire.

Watch out for people who disturb the peace in your church. Watch out for people who change the happy family environment, causing divisions and unhappiness in a place where there was only peace.

Some years ago, I organised a special fellowship for pastors and their wives. We would have this fellowship meeting in my home after church on Sundays. One day, a new pastor and his wife joined us for the fellowship. We enjoyed our time together, and decided to continue having this fellowship every week.

I clearly remember the day this new pastor made a comment about the fellowship. He said, "You people are blessed because you are able to eat chicken every day." He went on and made a comment about the things that he had seen in our fridge. Although it seemed like a joke, I took note of his comment. I began to notice a spirit of discontentment and comparison that we had never experienced before.

You see, we had had this fellowship for some years before this fellow came along. We were all happy together and no one was comparing what the other person had in his fridge. That was the beginning of discontentment and strife. Eventually, this pastor (who said he was not so fortunate to be able to eat chicken every day) became a source of great confusion, strife and rebellion. That is what it means to have a devil in your midst! A devil is someone who starts quarrels and confusion about nothing.

Watch out for people who change a happy fellowship into a centre of strife! Watch out for discontented people! Watch out for people who do not appreciate where they are and what they have. Instead of this fellow being appreciative that he was a guest in my home, he was busy analysing the items in my fridge! Watch out for the devil!

Satan did not appreciate the opportunity that he had to be in heaven. Satan did not appreciate the position that he had been given. He started a rebellion and introduced fighting and confusion in heaven.

All quarrels, battles and wars are caused by spirits of devils who go out to make people battle against each other. Notice the verse below. Spirits of devils go out into the earth to gather people to battle.

For they are THE SPIRITS OF DEVILS, working miracles, which go forth unto the kings of the earth and of the whole world, TO GATHER THEM TO THE BATTLE of that great day of God Almighty.

Revelation 16:14

People who do not want to end quarrels are those who are inspired by Satan. Hitler refused to end the Second World War, even though he had clearly lost. This was one of the clearest signs of Satanic influence on Hitler. He fought, so that any and every thing would be destroyed! He even wanted his own people, his own nation and every building in his country to be destroyed. Amazing! This is great evidence of the Satanic inspiration of the Second World War that caused the deaths of fifty million people.

Satan is the great inspirer of all wars. The sin of starting quarrels and wars is one of the favourite activities of the devil. A study of war reveals how senseless a war often is. No side really wins a war. Satan is very good at causing people to go to war. The history of mankind is the history of war. Television channels that purport to be showing history, basically show one war after another. Satan was thrown out of heaven because he incited a war in a place that was peaceful. There had never been anything like war in heaven. Satan started it all!

Until you have lived in a country that is destroyed by war, you will not understand the senselessness of war. Entire nations are destroyed for decades by a single war. Satan is the one who inspires people to do what will lead to their own destruction.

Today, there are people who bring war into places of peace. Peaceful families, peaceful churches, peaceful homes are turned into conflict zones because of the presence of men who walk in the sins of Satan. Watch out for pastors, leaders and workers who bring quarrels and conflict into a very peaceful fellowship.

Where do the senseless quarrels in our world come from? What was the outcome of the First World War? Before the First World War, many young men were eager to go to war because they had delusions of a grand conquest. Unfortunately, the First World War dragged on and became a senseless conflict, resulting in millions dying. What was the outcome of the Second World War? The Second World War killed over fifty million people and achieved nothing. Every country retained its old borders. No country gained anything from the war.

The outcome of these world wars reveals how an evil mind can orchestrate the conflicts of our world. The scripture above describes how the spirits of devils go out and gather the kings of the earth to battle. Devils are the spiritual beings that go out into the world to incite wars. All conflicts and quarrels are caused by Satan.

Where do many senseless quarrels come from? Sometimes, there are lovely couples who suit each other and yet have meaningless, mindless and senseless conflicts for years on end. These senseless quarrels divide the family and destroy its happiness.

Sometimes, couples separate and live in loneliness for the rest of their lives when they could have been happy with each other. It is almost impossible to understand how couples that look so beautiful on their wedding day can fight so much and even kill each other. The scripture above has clearly revealed that the originator of these terrible conflicts is the devil.

Watch out for people who start conflicts and refuse to back down. Men, like Hitler, who intentionally started conflicts and wars and caused the deaths of millions of people were clearly inspired by Satan.

Do not be drawn into battle

And I saw three unclean spirits like frogs come out of the mouth of the dragon, and out of the mouth of the beast, and out of the mouth of the false prophet.

For they are the spirits of devils, working miracles, which go forth unto the kings of the earth and of the whole world, TO GATHER THEM TO THE BATTLE of that great day of God Almighty.

Revelation 16:13-14

Satan wishes to draw you into a battle. Satan desires for you to have a conflict with your husband, your wife, your pastor, your friend, your family, your employee and your child. Do not allow yourself to be gathered to any battle! The devil is ready to gather you to a battle if you will yield yourself. If you do not recognize the opportunity to quarrel as what it really is, you will be drawn by the devil into many foolish fights.

When you deal with strife, quarrels and conflicts, you are dealing with Satan himself. When you allow strife and quarrels to flourish around you, you are allowing demonic activity to flourish. It is a great mistake to allow yourself to be drawn into conflicts. Deal with the devil by dealing properly with anything that draws you into conflict.

Wherever There is Conflict, There are Demons

Strife, quarrelling and wars are demonic in their very nature.

But if ye have bitter envying and STRIFE in your hearts, glory not, and lie not against the truth. This wisdom descendeth not from above, but is earthly, sensual, DEVILISH.

James 3:14-15

Some people have conflict with their leaders and are unable to maintain a peaceful, harmonious atmosphere in their ministry. Others have conflict in their marriages and are unable to have a single day of peace. There is always a quarrel, a problem or some cause of unhappiness in the relationship.

Persistent conflict in your life reveals the presence and activity of demonic creatures. You may never have a vision in which you actually see the devil sitting or standing in your room. But it is the devil that gathers people together for battle.

Demons Cause Conflicts Between Husband and Wife

I know at least two different pastors who were having constant conflicts with their wives and had visions where the presence of a demonic creature was uncovered. These supernatural visions and revelations helped the pastors to recognise that their marital conflicts were being orchestrated by the presence of an evil spirit.

When you know something is being organised against you in the spirit realm, you do not allow yourself to fall for it. Both of these ministers of the gospel immediately stopped quarrelling with their wives and earnestly tried to reconcile so that they would not fulfil the wishes of these devils that had gathered husband and wife together for battle.

It is the devil who gathers different parties together to fight foolish and senseless wars. You must be alert and conscious of the possibility that you have been gathered together to have a senseless battle or conflict with someone important in your life.

The Second World War caused the deaths of fifty million people. It was a senseless conflict and it achieved nothing. Millions of lives were destroyed but nothing was achieved. The only explanation for these useless fights is that armies were gathered together and set at each other's throats by a demon spirit. This is why you must deal with conflict, quarrels and strife by dealing with the devil himself. God has given you relationships that you must keep for the rest of your life. Do not allow the devil to break up the most important relationships of your life.

CHAPTER 9

The Sins of a Devil: Opposing God's Servants

Be sober, be vigilant; because YOUR ADVERSARY THE DEVIL, as a roaring lion, walketh about, seeking whom he may devour:

1 Peter 5:8

"**O**ne of you is a devil!"

How can you know when someone is a devil?

When somebody is a devil, he behaves exactly like the devil and opposes everything just as the devil does! The devil is the adversary. To be an adversary is to be an opposer.

When you deal with opposition in the ministry, you are dealing with Satan. When you allow opposers, hinderers, obstructors, adversaries and negative people to run free in your church, you are allowing the devil to feel free in your life and ministry.

It is a great mistake for you to allow someone to oppose you constantly. Deal with the devil by dealing properly with obstruction, opposition and the things that slow you down!

Where there is Opposition there is a Devil

Satan is an opposer. The word 'adversary' means an opposer. An opposer is someone who makes it difficult for you to progress, someone who stops you in your tracks. An adversary is someone who makes you go much slower than you ought to. Through an opposer, the devil finds a launching pad from which he can slow you down.

An adversary is someone who diverts you from your intended course. If you live and work with people who complain and grumble about you, you are living and working in the presence of opposing devils.

To anoint means to empower and inspire a person. When Satan empowers someone and inspires him to oppose you, you will struggle to accomplish your goals. People who are anointed by the devil to oppose you are usually people who have access to you. They are in strategic positions and their action or inaction makes life difficult for you.

An assistant pastor can become the greatest opposition to your life and ministry. It takes discernment and boldness to identify what is happening to you. Your wife can also become the devil to you. It will take grace, discernment and boldness to identify your spouse as the devil. It will take great boldness to rebuke your own wife as though you were rebuking the devil.

Jesus did exactly that when He sensed the opposer speaking through Peter. Peter was His closest and most trusted assistant. That is the position a wife, an assistant pastor or a key administrator occupies. Peter tried to block Jesus and prevent Him from going to the cross. But Jesus threw him aside immediately.

But he turned, and said unto Peter, GET THEE BEHIND ME, SATAN: thou art an offence unto me: for thou savourest not the things that be of God, but those that be of men.

Matthew 16:23

One day, a minister of the gospel was waiting on God in his church building. He was the pastor of a church that was not growing. This is a church that was known for conflict, confusion and quarrels. One afternoon, as the pastor paced up and down in the empty hall, he looked up at the ceiling and it just seemed to disappear. Within the rafters of the ceiling was a monkey. The pastor's eyes had been opened and he was seeing in the spirit realm. To his amazement, there was this creature that lived in the ceiling of his church building. The pastor rebuked the demon and it fell to the ground. He commanded the evil spirit to go out of the building, which it did.

And what was the effect of this evil spirit being dislodged from the ceiling rafters? A year later, the evil atmosphere of the church: the confusion, complaining, grumbling, quarrelling was no more and the church grew considerably.

You see, this evil spirit was opposing the peace and the growth of the church. It was the presence of this devil that ensured that the pastor's vision for church growth was not accomplished. Every pastor must be sensitive and discerning. You must be able to detect the presence and activity of subtle opposition that slows you down. When you detect opposition, you are actually detecting the presence of demon spirits.

Even if you do not have a fantastic vision like this one, *you can know that there is demon activity by the presence of persistent opposition, frustration and slowing down of your vision.* Persistent opposition to your vision, your dreams and your calling is a sign that there are demon powers released specifically against you.

Rise up now in the name of Jesus. It is time to expose and uncover the invisible opposer in your life and ministry. It is time to overturn, overrule and arrest the activities of opposition spirits.

I command all spiritual monkeys, spiritual apes and other spiritual birds to leave your residence and your church! I take authority over all spiritual insects and spiritual fishes from the dark world! Your day to shine has come! You will never be held back any more. Within three months of reading these pages, you will see a permanent change in your ministry! Indeed, you will never be found at the same spot again after today!

CHAPTER 10

The Sins of a Devil: Misleading the Masses

Now the serpent was more subtil than any beast of the field which the Lord God had made. And he said unto the woman, Yea, hath God said, ye shall not eat of every tree of the garden?

And the woman said unto the serpent, we may eat of the fruit of the trees of the garden:

But of the fruit of the tree which is in the midst of the garden, God hath said, Ye shall not eat of it, neither shall ye touch it, lest ye die.

AND THE SERPENT SAID UNTO THE WOMAN, YE SHALL NOT SURELY DIE . . . .

And the Lord God said, Behold, the man is become as one of us, to know good and evil: and now, lest he put forth his hand, and take also of the tree of life, and eat, and live for ever:

Therefore the Lord God sent him forth from the garden of Eden, to till the ground from whence he was taken.

Genesis 3:1-4, 22-23

"One of you is a devil!"

How can you know when someone is a devil?

When somebody is a devil, he behaves exactly like the devil and misleads the masses just as the devil did!

There was a pastor who was put in charge of a church for eight weeks. He was put in charge of this church because the senior pastor had to travel with his family for some weeks.

When the senior pastor came back from his trip in Europe, the pastor in charge had decided to leave the church. The senior pastor was surprised at the sudden decision of this pastor to leave. Even then, he did not know what was about to hit him.

When the pastor resigned, he took along with him the entire church. The senior pastor was left with twenty members whilst three thousand members followed the breakaway pastor. This pastor had inspired three thousand members to leave their home church and their senior pastor to follow him.

Satan is the one who misleads the masses. Through fine speeches, enticing words and empty talk, Satan misled Adam and Eve and destroyed the rest of the human race. The sin of misleading the masses is the single most destructive activity of the devil. The entire world has been destroyed by Satan's false offer of *promotion, independence and equality* with God.

Today, Satan is making this same offer through some pastors, politicians and leaders. *Promotion, independence and equality!* That really sounds exciting! Very few people can resist fine speeches and nice-sounding words. Watch out for people who are walking in the very same sins of Satan. They come and present these three offers *(promotion, independence and equality)* to anyone who is simple-minded.

When pastors are breaking away from churches, they entice Christians and the main church with this offer: "You will be promoted! You will have your independence! You will be equal to them! You will be a pastor in the new church. You will be promoted. You will be free from the rules and regulations of the old church. You will be equal to the old church." Wow, what an offer! *Promotion, independence and equality!*

Lucifer misled Adam and Eve and destroyed the human race. Satan offered Adam and Eve independence, promotion and equality with God.

It is easy to see that the human race is a destroyed race of beings. The whole world is racing towards a cataclysmic conclusion. It is most likely that our nuclear weapons will soon be deployed against each other. Who introduced all the evil that we have in this world? Did God create the world in this way? No!

When a snake bites a man, he may hang in the balance between life and death for several weeks. Indeed, when a snake bites a person, he can go into a life-threatening condition and need intensive care. When Satan *"bites"* a church, the whole church runs amok. Everything is destroyed and nothing is the same again. A church's life can hang in the balance because of a little Satanic *"bite"*. Satan deceived Adam and Eve who then left the garden and walked out of a blessed life and into a cursed existence.

Adam and Eve lived to regret having followed the deception of Satan. Look at how they must have lamented after the fall. These pitiful narrations are excerpts from a Christian book called *"The First Book of Adam and Eve"*[1] ;

[2] Then Adam stood up in the cave and said, "O God, why has light departed from us and darkness covered us? Why did you leave us in this extensive darkness? Why do you plague us like this?

And this darkness, O Lord, where was it before it covered us? It is because of this that we cannot see each other.

1.Lumpkin, J. (2010) *The Encyclopedia of Lost and Rejected Scriptures: The Pseudepigrapha and Apocrypha* 1 ed. Blountsville, Ala.: Fifth Estate.

For so long as we were in the garden we neither saw nor even knew what darkness was. I was not hidden from Eve, neither was she hidden from me, until now that she cannot see me and darkness came over us to separate us from each other.

But she and I were both in one bright light. I saw her and she saw me. Yet now since we came into this cave darkness has covered us and separated us from each other so that I do not see her, and she does not see me."

Chapter XII: 7-10

Then Adam said to God, "I dry up in the heat, I am faint from walking, and I don't want to be in this world. And I don't know when You will let me rest and take me out of it."

Then the Lord God said to him, "O Adam, it cannot be now, not until you have ended your days. Then I shall bring you out of this miserable land."

And Adam said to God, "While I was in the garden I knew neither heat, nor fatigue, neither transience, nor trembling, nor fear; but now since I came to this land, all this affliction has come over me.

Then God said to Adam, "So long as you were keeping My commandment, My light and My grace rested on you. But when you transgressed My commandment, sorrow and misery came to you in this land."

And Adam cried and said, "O Lord, do not cut me off for this, neither punish me with heavy plagues, nor yet repay me according to my sin; for we, of our own will, transgressed Your commandment and ignored Your law and tried to become gods like you when Satan the enemy deceived us."

Chapter XXII: 1-5

Then Adam said to God, "O Lord, You created us, and made us fit to be in the garden; and before I transgressed, You

55

made all beasts come to me, that I should name them. Your grace was then on me; and I named every one according to Your mind; and you made them all subject to me.

But now, O Lord God, that I have transgressed Your commandment, all beasts will rise against me and will devour me, and Eve Your handmaid; and will cut off our life from the face of the earth.

I therefore beg you, O God, that since You have made us come out of the garden, and have made us be in a strange land, You will not let the beasts hurt us."

Chapter VII: 3-6

Then Adam cried and said, "O God, when we lived in the garden, and our hearts were lifted up, we saw the angels that sang praises in heaven, but now we can't see like we once saw. No. When we entered the cave all creation became hidden from us."

Then God the Lord said to Adam, "When you were under subjection to Me, you had a bright nature within you and for that reason could you see distant things. But after you transgressed your bright nature was taken out of you and it was not left in you to see distant things, but only things near to you, as is the ability of the flesh, for it is brutish."

Chapter VIII:1-2 [2]

Do not allow Satan to deceive you as he deceived Adam and Eve. Satan is a master of dangling illusions before our eyes. Do not follow vain things! Do not follow lying promises! Do not follow the masses! Do not follow shiny things that look good. Look not on the outward appearance but think carefully before you follow any Satanic leadings. Watch out for the devil! He is real!

[2-2] Ibid.

CHAPTER 11

The Sins of a Devil: Being a Liar

Ye are of your father the devil, and the lusts of your father ye will do. He was a murderer from the beginning, and abode not in the truth, because THERE IS NO TRUTH IN HIM. When he speaketh a lie, he speaketh of his own: for HE IS A LIAR, and the father of it.

John 8:44

W

hen you deal with deception, you are dealing with Satan himself. When you allow liars to run free in your life, you are allowing the devil to feel free in your life and ministry. It is a great mistake for you to allow liars to flourish around you. Deal with the devil by dealing properly with lies!

Where There Are Liars There Are Demons

Wherever you find deception and lies you can safely assume that there has been an infiltration of demons. Many of us pastors have allowed evil spirits into our ministries because of the lies we tell.

One day, a pastor was unwell and unable to honour an invitation to preach. He called up the one who had invited him and explained that he would not be able to come. Then he asked the host to please tell the congregation that he had travelled to Europe for an emergency meeting and that is why he would not be able to make it. But this was a lie. There was no need to deceive the congregation about having had to make an emergency trip to Europe. Telling lies is a sign of the infiltration of evil spirits into your life.

On another occasion I was with a man of God who had ministered in many different parts of the world. Somehow, I felt that there was something wrong with his ministry. But I could not place my finger on what was wrong with this ministry. As I pondered over it, the Lord showed me one simple thing.

He said, "Think about how many lies this man of God has told since you got close to him." As I thought over this, I realised that this man of God had said several things that were not accurate. He had also made several promises that he did not keep. I knew many Christians who had been upset because this man of God had made promises to them that he had not kept.

The presence of untruths, half-truths, failed promises and failure to keep agreements was evident. Suddenly, I knew what the Lord was showing me. There was some kind of infiltration of demonic activity in this great man of God's life and ministry.

The scripture that Satan is the father of lies is something you must not take lightly. Lies are significant because Satan is the father of lies. If you see a child walking on the street, you can assume that the father of the child is nearby somewhere. When you see a lie, you should know that the father of lies is around. This is why the presence of lies indicates the presence of the devil. The father must be near the child!

Every single lie is authored, engineered, inspired and used by the devil himself. Satan is the father of lies! These are the words of Jesus! Ministers of the gospel must watch out and not allow demon activity to enter through lying and deception.

Many ministers allow evil spirits to gain access to their ministry when they start telling lies from the pulpit. It is common for us to exaggerate figures and make promises that we do not keep. It is common for us to fail to keep our word.

An even more common and dangerous practice is to preach a false gospel to mislead God's people from the truth of the Word of God. This practice opens great doors for senior evil spirits to infiltrate the ministry.

Strong deception is a hallmark of demon activity. Activities that involve a lot of lying and deception therefore have a lot of associated demonic activity.

Politicians also tell many lies. As such, there are a lot of evil spirits associated with political work. Many Christians fell into darkness when they got involved in politics. They were forced to sacrifice truth in order to be accepted in their political party. You will find born again Christians telling great lies and defending the indefensible just because they belong to a political party. This is how they open their lives to evil spirits.

Many financial institutions revolve around deception. Many bonds, stocks, investments and mortgages are heavily laced with deception in order to get people to entrust their money to them.

Remember this: wherever there is a liar there is a devil! When you are in the presence of a liar you are in the presence of a devil. And when you are in the presence of the devil you are in the presence of danger.

Satan is a liar: Liars are Destroyers

1. **The coming of a liar into your life is the coming of a devil.**

    The originator of every lie is Satan. One of Satan's sins is to lie. Anyone who tells lies is committing one of the sins of the devil. Satan is the father of all lies. A person lying to you, therefore, originates from Satan. There were no lies before the devil came into the world. When Satan speaks a lie, it comes from his very nature. When you hear a lie spoken, you are hearing something out of the very heart and nature of the devil.

    Ye are of your father the devil, and the lusts of your father ye will do. He was a murderer from the beginning, and abode not in the truth, because there is no truth in him. When he speaketh a lie, HE SPEAKETH OF HIS OWN: for he is a liar, and the father of it.

    John 8:44

    Satan's lies are so powerful that they have the ability to deceive the whole world. Imagine something that is so strong that it can mislead billions of people.

    And the great dragon was cast out, that old serpent, called the Devil, and Satan, which DECEIVETH THE WHOLE WORLD: he was cast out into the earth, and his angels were cast out with him.

    Revelation 12:9

60

Satan also manipulates deceptive circumstances. He is able to manipulate circumstances so that you will be deceived and follow them. These manipulated circumstances are called lying wonders.

Even him, whose coming is after the working of Satan with all power and signs and LYING WONDERS, And with all deceivableness of unrighteousness in them that perish; because they received not the love of the truth, that they might be saved.

2 Thessalonians 2:9-10

2. **The coming of a liar into your life is the coming of Satan and therefore the coming of imminent destruction.**

In the presence of a liar you are in the presence of the devil and in the presence of imminent destruction. When Adam was in the garden of Eden, he was in the presence of imminent destruction. Adam was in danger of destruction when the devil entered the garden.

The whole world stood under threat because a liar had entered the garden. The human race teetered in the balance because a liar was speaking to Eve.

When Jesus was in the presence of a liar in the wilderness, He was in the presence of danger and destruction. When Absalom tolerated the presence of Hushai as an adviser, he was in the presence of imminent destruction. Absalom was in danger of being captured and killed by king David's forces because he tolerated the lies of Hushai the Archite.

When Tamar accepted the person and presence of her brother who posed as someone who needed her nursing care, she was in imminent danger. She was in danger of being raped and being destroyed by her brother.

When Samson lay down to relax by a lying and deceptive Delilah, he was in great danger. He was in danger of blindness, captivity and death.

When Sisera relaxed in the presence of deceptive and beautiful Jael, he was in danger of a nail being hammered into his head.

Let us look through your life. Do you live with a liar? Does a liar work for you? In the presence of a liar, you are in the presence of a devil! In the presence of a liar you are in the presence of danger!

3.   **The coming of a liar into your life is the coming of Satan and therefore the coming of your punishment.**

One of God's punishments is to allow you to believe a lie. Your curse comes to you when a liar is sent to you. The coming of the liar with his lies is the coming of God's punishment into your life.

And for this cause GOD SHALL SEND THEM STRONG DELUSION, THAT THEY SHOULD BELIEVE A LIE: THAT THEY ALL MIGHT BE DAMNED who believed not the truth, but had pleasure in unrighteousness.

2 Thessalonians 2:11-12

4.   **The coming of a liar into your life is the coming of Satan and therefore the coming of a murderer.**

When you are in the presence of a liar you are in the presence of a disguised murderer. A liar is not what he appears to be. A liar will not do what he says he will do. A liar is not what he says he is. A liar is a murderer! A liar is a killer!

Ye are of your father the devil, and the lusts of your father ye will do. HE WAS A MURDERER from the beginning, and abode not in the truth, because there is no truth in him. When he speaketh a lie, he speaketh of his own: for HE IS A LIAR, and the father of it.

John 8:44

There are grades of liars and therefore there are grades of murderous capabilities. Not every liar can deceive the whole world. Some liars can deceive only a nation. Some liars can deceive a church. Some liars can deceive a pastor whilst some liars cannot. Some liars can deceive a husband, a wife or a whole community. Some liars can only deceive uneducated people, whilst others can deceive educated people as well. All liars are potential killers! All liars are potential murderers!

And the great dragon was cast out, that old serpent, called the Devil, and Satan, which deceiveth the whole world: he was cast out into the earth, and his angels were cast out with him.

Revelation 12:9

5.   **The coming of a liar into your life is the coming of Satan and therefore the coming of a pretender.**

A pretender needs to be a liar so that he can cover up for all the aspects of his life that are not real and that do not add up.

Lies and deception are often the only covering for past evils. Lies and deception are a pretender's protection. Lies and deception are the only foundation a pretender has to stand on to do further evil. Lies and deception are a clear foundation for betrayal.

CHAPTER 12

The Sins of a Devil: Separatism

And there was war in heaven: Michael and his angels fought against the dragon; and THE DRAGON FOUGHT AND HIS ANGELS,

Revelation 12:7

THESE BE THEY WHO SEPARATE THEMSELVES, sensual, having not the Spirit.

Jude 19

"**O**ne of you is a devil!"

How can you know when someone is a devil?

When somebody is a devil, he behaves exactly like the devil and becomes a separatist just as the devil was!

What does it mean to have a devil in your midst? It means to have a separatist in your midst. Separatism is perhaps the favourite sin of Satan! "Be separate, be independent and be your own man" is a favourite song inspired by Satan. Separating yourself from the rest and not being a part of the fellowship, is a basic Satanic manoeuvre. Satan did not want to be part of the heavenly community. He did not want to stay with the others. He wanted to be separate and on his own.

Until you have encountered "separatism" you will not know how disruptive, distracting and destructive it is. Separatism is the reason why people cannot build and prosper. Separatism is the reason why things that should grow large are still small. A basic deception is that *"I can do without you and you can do without me."* But this is not true because the Bible says we are perfected by each other.

God having provided some better thing for us, that THEY WITHOUT US SHOULD NOT BE MADE PERFECT.

Hebrews 11:40

The devil was thrown out of heaven because of this sin of separatism. Satan has inspired countless numbers of people to follow his example and walk in the sin of separatism. Many people are walking in the sins of Satan and continue to fight to be separate. Separatists deserve to be cast out and cast away forever. That is the only treatment a separatist deserves.

Separatism is destructive! Imagine if your arms decided to separate from your body. Imagine what it would be like if your two kidneys just took off, claiming that they were not called to be in your body! Imagine what would happen if your eyes wrote a letter of resignation, in the middle of your life, claiming that they had only intended to stay for twenty years?

Separatism is the evil of coming away from the rest of the family. Separatism is the tendency to break up the family by coming aside and staying aside. Separatism is the art of making yourself different and not wanting to be part of the group. Separatism is the art of abandoning loyalty for the sake of a personal vision.

Separatism is the art of being a special person who never wants to fit into the crowd.

Separatism is an evil tendency that comes into people when they are under Satan's influence. It is the nature of Satan to want to be separate. Even in heaven, in the midst of the glory, Satan desired to stand alone and separate himself from his fellow angels.

Satan was not impressed with the loyalty of the other angels. He saw no reason to continue staying in heaven to worship God. Satan saw no reason to say good things about God. But there were angels who disagreed with him and fought against him. God almighty did not need to fight Satan.

It was a war between fellow angels.

It was a war between the loyal angels and the disloyal angels.

It was a war between angels who loved God and angels who criticised God.

Satan committed the first sin of separatism! Satan has been inspiring many others to be separatists!

Judas and Separatism

Jesus answered them, Have not I chosen you twelve, and one of you is a devil?

John 6:70

When you deal with separatism, you are dealing with Satan himself. When you allow disloyal people to run free in your church, you are allowing the devil to feel free in your life and ministry.

What is a real life encounter with someone? It is an encounter in which you actually meet a person, talk to a person and even touch a person. Most people expect to encounter the devil in the form of a reddish creature with a spear and two large horns. But a real life encounter with the devil is probably taking place in your life today without you realising it.

Jesus said that Judas was a devil! I did not say that Judas was a devil. Jesus said that Judas was a devil! Jesus Christ encountered Satan when he encountered Judas. Jesus Christ encountered a separatist when He encountered Judas. You are encountering Satan in a real and living way when you encounter a Judas.

The scripture is very clear that Jesus Christ called Judas a devil. Someone who betrays you and is disloyal to you is a living, palpable human devil. I did not write the Bible. If Jesus called Judas a devil, why would you call him anything else? Judas is famous for his treachery, disloyalty and betrayal. Satan betrayed the trust and position that was given to him. Judas did to Jesus exactly what Satan did when he rebelled in heaven. He betrayed the great trust and position that was given to him.

Evil spirits are in operation when someone is betraying you, turning against you and separating from you. That is the work of the devil. Satan is the originator of disloyal and treacherous behaviour. Lucifer was the leader of the rebellious and fallen angels who left their first estate and separated from God. "And the angels which kept not their first estate, but left their own habitation, he hath reserved in everlasting chains under darkness unto the judgment of the great day" (Jude 1:6).

Since then, Satan has been inspiring people to rebel against their leaders. Satan (who was disloyal to God who appointed him) has been inspiring others to be disloyal to those who appointed them.

Any time you find people ganging up against the leader, forming parties, groups, murmuring, conspiring and standing against the authority over their lives, Satan is at work.

Sometimes, people are disloyal through their ignorance and naïveté. Two hundred people followed Absalom when he rose up to fight against his own father. However, these two hundred people rebelled in the innocence of their mind.

And with Absalom went two hundred men out of Jerusalem, that were called; and they went IN THEIR SIMPLICITY, and they knew not any thing

2 Samuel 15:11

If you are struggling in your church to gain the absolute trust of your associates and elders, you must think of demon activity. Devils are working where there is disloyalty and treachery.

Some years ago, I was the pastor of a local church. One day, I had a vision and saw myself in a boxing ring, boxing away against an opponent. I suddenly realized who I was fighting with - a prominent lady and church member. The Lord revealed to me that this person and some others were fighting against me with their tongues. This vision was a God-given glimpse into the spirit world. It was clearly revealed to me that someone and something was fighting against me.

Satan is the author of all forms of separation and disloyalty. Most pastors are looking out for devils in witches. They expect to see the devil in an old wizened lady who lives alone in a haunted house. They say to themselves, "This is the witch in the church." But the devil comes as an angel of light! Most of the devils operate through nice-looking people.

Watch out, dear friend! The constant breaking up of your church, separation of pastors from the leadership, the division and confusion in your church is a sign of the presence and activities of devils. Perhaps, it is a specific demon spirit that is harassing your church. Usually it is a demon gang that is at work against the ministry. Evil spirits hardly work alone. Rise up and deal with the devils that have besieged your ministry!

Deal with all disloyal separatists in exactly the same way that God dealt with Satan. Throw them out! Don't have any more meetings with them! Don't discuss their ideas and visions with them! Read all about loyalty and disloyalty in my book. Learn to destroy the power of disloyalty and separatism through the key of knowledge.

CHAPTER 13

The Sins of a Devil: Independence

For thou hast said in thine heart, I will ascend into heaven, I will exalt my throne above the stars of God: I will sit also upon the mount of the congregation, in the sides of the north: I will ascend above the heights of the clouds; I will be like the most High.

Isaiah 14:13-14

"**O**ne of you is a devil!"

How can you know when someone is a devil?

When somebody is a devil, he behaves exactly like the devil and fights for an inappropriate and evil independence just as the devil did!

Satan is the great inspirer of all forms of premature independence. The sin of independence before the right time is one of the most destructive activities of devils. Until you have lived in a country that gained independence long before the people were ready to govern themselves, you will not understand the effects of premature independence.

Entire nations are destroyed by that single act of "independence before time". Imagine a baby in the womb that cries for independence whilst it is connected by the umbilical cord. That baby is calling for its own death! Satan inspires people to call out for their own premature death.

Do you remember the mad man of Gadara and how he cut himself with stones? He cut himself and hurt himself because he was inspired by Satan. Satan is the one who inspires people to hurt themselves! Satan is the one who inspires people to do what will lead to their own destruction!

Today, many people are walking in the sins of Satan and being inspired to fight for independence which will only lead to their destruction. Pastors are inspired to be independent when they cannot lead themselves! Churches are inspired to be independent when they cannot govern themselves! Nations are inspired to be independent when they do not know anything about leadership and government! Watch out for people who stand up in the name of independence but are actually rebels.

Satan attempted to be independent from God. However, no one can be independent from God. You want to be on your own because you think you do not need God's input. You also think you can run your life as well as God can run it for you. In fact, you even think you can do a better job at running your own affairs than God can. Independence is often a fruit of pride.

The voice of independence is often the voice of pride. If you are used to it, you will soon recognize it when you hear it. This is what it sounds like:

"I want to be on my own!"

"I don't want to be under you!"

"I don't want to work for anyone!"

"I am as good as you are!"

"Why should I work for you when I can work for myself?"

"I don't want to serve anyone!"

"I have my own calling!"

"I have my own ministry!"

"I have heard from God myself!"

"I don't need you!"

"I don't need you and you don't need me."

"I don't want to be associated with you!"

"I don't *need* to be associated with you!"

"I will prove to you and to everyone that I am called and anointed!"

"I am my own man!"

"You were not there when God called me!"

"I can make it without you."

"I will make it without you or anyone else."

Notice how many times Satan used the word "I". Satan was independently promoting himself, exalting himself, and declaring his personal ambitions. He was doing this whether anyone joined him or not.

This is the attitude of evil independence that seeks to be separate, isolated, and have its own vision. A separate, unique and different vision (*I will ascend...*) always leads to division. This is the original sin of Satan and it is the sin of many men today. They want to be independent of God. All attempts to be independent from God are inspired by the devil. No part of creation is independent of God. God sends the water from heaven and causes the grass to grow. The trees, the birds and the hills are dependent on God for instructions on what to do. Even the lions look to God for their meals. "O Lord, how manifold are thy works! In wisdom hast thou made them all: the earth is full of thy riches" (Psalm 104:24). It is only the wickedness of the devil and the wickedness of man that seeks to be independent of God.

He watereth the hills from his chambers: the earth is satisfied with the fruit of thy works. He causeth the grass to grow for the cattle, and herb for the service of man: that he may bring forth food out of the earth; And wine that maketh glad the heart of man, and oil to make his face to shine, and bread which strengtheneth man's heart.

The trees of the Lord are full of sap; the cedars of Lebanon, which he hath planted;

Where the birds make their nests: as for the stork, the fir trees are her house.

The high hills are a refuge for the wild goats; and the rocks for the conies.

He appointed the moon for seasons: the sun knoweth his going down.

Thou makest darkness, and it is night: wherein all the beasts of the forest do creep forth. THE YOUNG

LIONS ROAR AFTER THEIR PREY, AND SEEK THEIR MEAT FROM GOD.

Psalm 104:13-21

Ideologies that Eliminate God

All ideologies that elevate man to the point where he thinks that he does not need God are Satanically inspired. It is only Satan who inspires you to separate yourself from God. The theories of humanism, secularism and rationalism make man feel that he does not need God. They are filled with the inspiration of Satan. Satan only wants man to be independent of God. Satan suggested that to Eve. That is how come we are in this big mess today!

Humanism: is a line of thinking that attaches prime importance to human rather than divine things.

[1]*Secularism:* is a system of ideas that disregard or reject any form of religious faith and worship. Its primary objective is the total elimination of all religious elements from society. Secularism ensures that the right of individuals to freedom of religion is always balanced by the right to be free from religion. Secularists believe that man is the measure of all things, that morals are man-centered, not God-centered.[1]

Rationalism: is the practice of accepting reason as the supreme authority rather than a religious belief.

Most of the wars in this world are caused by a desire to be independent. Therefore, many deaths in our world are caused indirectly by the spirit of independence. Look at this amazing list of wars that have been fought over the years. All these wars were fought for independence. Can you imagine the millions of people that have died in our world just because of the fight for independence?

Wars of Independence in the World[2]

1521-1523	Swedish War of Liberation from the Kalmar Union
1568-1648	Eighty Years' War - Independence of the Netherlands from Spain
1640-1668	Portuguese Restoration War – Restoration of Portuguese independence from Spain
1703-1711	Rakoczi's War of Independence – Limited Autonomy for Hungary
1775-1783	American Revolutionary War – Independence of United States from Great Britain
1791-1804	Haitian Revolution - Independence of Haiti from France
1804-1813	First Serbian Uprising – Defeat of Insurgents
1808-1814	Peninsular War – Independence of Spain from France
1810s-1820s	Latin American Wars of Independence from Spain (Argentina, Bolivia, Chile, Ecuador, Mexico, Peru, Venezuela)
1821-1827	Greek War of Independence from the Ottoman Empire
1830-1839	Belgian Revolution – Independence of Belgium from Netherlands
1835-1836	Texas Revolution – Independence of Texas from Mexico
1843-1849	Dominican War of Independence from Haiti
1848	First Italian War of Independence – Italian unification not achieved
1857-1858	Indian Rebellion of 1857 – Indian insurgents defeated by Great Britain
1859	Second Italian War of Independence – Not successful

1861-1864	American Civil War - Attempt by Confederate States to be independent of the United States
1863-1865	January Uprising – Defeat of Polish insurgents by Russia
1866	Third Italian War of Independence – Austrian empire loses Veneto to Kingdom of Italy
1876	April Uprising – Led to the independence of Bulgaria from the Ottoman Empire in 1878
1877	Romanian War of Independence from the Ottoman Empire
1896-1898	Philippine Revolution – Philippine failed to achieve independence
1899-1913	Philippine-American War – Defeat of insurgents by United States
1916-1918	Arab Revolt – defeat of Arab aspirations for independence by post -World War 1 partition
1917-1921	Ukrainian War of Independence from Russia
1918-1920	Estonia war of Independence from the Russian Empire
1918-1920	Latvian war of Independence from the Russian Empire
1918-1920	Lithuanian war of Independence from the Russian Empire and Poland
1919-1921	Irish War of Independence – secession of 26 of Ireland's 32 counties from the United Kingdom
1920-1926	Rif War – Spain retains control of Spanish Morocco
1945-1949	Indonesian National Revolution – Independence of Indonesia from the Netherlands
1946-1954	First Indochina War – Independence of Vietnam, Laos, and Cambodia from France.
1948	Arab-Israeli War – Israel defeated Arabs and retained its independence

1952-1960	Kenyan Mau Mau Uprising – Defeat of insurgents by United Kingdom
1954-1962	Algerian War of Independence from France
1961-1974	Angolan War of Independence from Portugal
1961-1991	Eritrean War of Independence from Ethiopia
1963-1974	Guinea-Bissau War of Independence from Portugal
1964-1974	Mozambican War of Independence from Portugal
1966-1988	Namibian War of Independence from South Africa
1967-1970	Nigerian Civil War – Defeat and dissolution of the Republic of Biafra
1971	Bangladesh Liberation War of Independence from Pakistan
1983-2005	Second Sudanese Civil War – South Sudan's attempt to be independent of Sudan
1991-1995	Croatian war - Independence from Yugoslavia
1991	Ten-Day War - Independence of Slovenia from Yugoslavia
1992-1995	Bosnian War – Independence of Bosnia from Yugoslavia
1996-1999	Kosovo War – No legal changes to Yugoslav borders but political separation of Kosovo from the rest of Yugoslavia
2012	Tuareg (Northern Mali) rebellion – Attempt by Azawad to be independent of Mali

In the church, many have become a sad version of what they were called to be because they desired independence so badly. Many times it is better to be the leg of an elephant than to be the head of an ant.

There are many small churches, which are inspired to be independent rather than to be a part of a fellowship. There are many independent churches that need to be dependent and part of a fellowship.

Satanic infiltration is growing in the last days, and therefore more independence is sought. For instance, in 1946 only 4% of all Pentecostal churches were independent, in both the United States and Canada. Today, much more than 75% of Pentecostal churches are single independent churches.

Most older churches were part of a denomination! For instance, in 1946, in an area where there were 27 Pentecostal churches, 26 of them were an integral part of a denomination.

Unfortunately, as Satanic infiltration occurs, more and more independence is sought. Satan causes pride and independence to grow in the hearts of men of God. Everyone wants to be independent and everyone wants to be the head. Satan is the author of evil and inappropriate independence. Satan is the father of the children of pride.

He (Leviathan) beholdeth all high things: he is a king over all the children of pride.

Job 41:34

CHAPTER 14

The Sins of a Devil: Weakening Nations

How art thou fallen from heaven, O Lucifer, son of the morning!

How art thou cut down to the ground, WHICH DIDST WEAKEN THE NATIONS! ... They that see thee shall narrowly look upon thee, and consider thee, saying,

Is this the man that made the earth to tremble, that did shake kingdoms;

That MADE THE WORLD AS A WILDERNESS, AND DESTROYED THE CITIES thereof; that opened not the house of his prisoners?

Isaiah 14:12, 16-17

"**O**ne of you is a devil!"

How can you know when someone is a devil?

When somebody is a devil, he behaves exactly like the devil and weakens nations, churches and families just as the devil did!

One of the dreadful activities of the devil is the sin of weakening nations. The sin of weakening nations has introduced great turmoil into the world. Until you have travelled through the many failed states in Africa that have no real government, no security or development, you will not know how devastating this activity of Satan is. The devil was thrown out of heaven because he wanted to turn heaven into a "failed state". He wanted to turn heaven into a centre of chaos and make it into a wilderness. Satan has inspired countless human beings to be senseless destroyers of their countries. Many leaders have risen up and destroyed their nations. Adolf Hitler weakened Germany by leading his country into six years of chaos, confusion and war. Millions of people died senselessly as they followed his leadership.

Many people are walking in the sins of Satan and continuing in the work of weakening nations and turning nations into wildernesses. Watch out for nation destroyers! Watch out for political parties and fatally deficient leaders who lead their countries astray until there is no safety, no security, no water, no light, no good schools, no good hospitals, no jobs, no roads, no development, no industries and no peace.

Satan has destroyed nations. Instead of strong countries without hunger, starvation, poverty and sickness, the earth is filled with weak nations that struggle on the brink of bankruptcy, starvation and war.

Most nations are in one crisis or another and many nations are failed states. Many nations have no real government. Many nations cannot govern themselves and cannot feed themselves. The weakened state of nations of our world is caused by Satan's presence in the governments that rule the nations.

Many governments commit the sins of the devil and weaken the nations which they rule. This is why it is important to pray for our leaders. The princes of the nation fight for control over the souls and hearts of our politicians. Princes over the nations seek to direct the leaders of the nations to destroy their nations.

Imagine a head of state whose aim is to spread homosexuality before he leaves office. Imagine a head of state who leads his country into war! Imagine a head of state who drives his country into irrecoverable debts! Imagine a head of state who destroys the educational system of an entire nation! Imagine a head of state who steals all the money of his country and stashes it away in a secret account! Imagine a head of state who destroys the health system of his country!

It is Satan who is the destroyer of this world. Men who have received the nature of Satan and have become living devils also walk in these same sins to destroy this world.

Watch out for men who help Satan to weaken and destroy nations through corruption, war and bad leadership. Many politicians have evil spirits in them and carry out the plan of Satan to destroy nations. God is going to punish Satan and all those who follow his ways of destroying this earth.

And the nations were angry, and thy wrath is come, and the time of the dead, that they should be judged, and that thou shouldest give reward unto thy servants the prophets, and to the saints, and them that fear thy name, small and great; and SHOULDEST DESTROY THEM WHICH DESTROY THE EARTH.

Revelation 11:18

Our world is gradually being turned into a wilderness of dirty places, filthy cities destroyed jungles, destroyed lakes, filthy beaches and polluted rivers. The sea is full of the dead bodies of mankind and the nuclear wastes of our world. The deserts have spread to areas they were never intended to be because of the greedy and wicked deforestation activities of men.

Many rivers can no longer be used for drinking because they are polluted with cyanide and other metals. Through the greed of mankind, many of the wild animals are near extinction. Our world is gradually turning into a wilderness. It is a far cry from its original state. This is why it is wonderful to visit places where nature has been preserved, where Satan has not been able to destroy. Satan has truly weakened the nations of this world. This is one of his sins and he will pay for destroying this world! Every man who rises up to destroy the world through his leadership is walking in the sins of Satan and is being a devil to his nation!

CHAPTER 15

The Sins of a Devil: Tempting God's Servants

Then was Jesus led up of the Spirit into the wilderness to be tempted of the devil.

Matthew 4:1

"Oｎ

ne of you is a devil!"

How can you know when someone is a devil?

When somebody is a devil, he behaves exactly like the devil and tempts God's servants just as the devil did!

Temptation is a sign of the devil's presence. Persistent repeated temptations are sure signs of evil spirits in your life. Jesus Christ was tempted in the wilderness. Jesus Christ was tempted by the devil and not by God!

One of the great sins of Satan was his attempt to destroy the Son of God through temptation. How could he try to make the Son of God fall into sin? How could he create a trap for Jesus Christ? How dare he lay a trap for the Lord instead of laying a table for Him and ministering to Him! What a wicked disrespectful creature Satan is!

And when the tempter came to him, he said, If thou be the Son of God, command that these stones be made bread....

And saith unto him, IF THOU BE THE SON OF GOD, CAST THYSELF DOWN: for it is written, He shall give his angels charge concerning thee: and in their hands they shall bear thee up, lest at any time thou dash thy foot against a stone.

Matthew 4:3, 6

However, a few years later, He was tempted with exactly the same test – to prove that He was the Son of God. Men, acting as devils, cried out to Him on the cross, urging Him to show that He was the Son of God. The same devil who tempted Him in the wilderness had come back to tempt Him whilst He was on the cross.

And they that passed by reviled him, wagging their heads, and saying, Thou that destroyest the temple, and buildest it in three days, save thyself. IF THOU

BE THE SON OF GOD, COME DOWN FROM THE CROSS.

Matthew 27:39-40

Tempting men and causing them to fall through their weaknesses and fleshly desires is a hallmark of Satan's wickedness. Satan is the tempter. All temptations you have ever encountered are inspired by the devil. Satan desperately wants you to fall. As long as you are upright and moral he has no access to your life.

One of the reasons for temptation is to open you up to other unrelated evil spirits. One thing leads to another and one evil spirit opens the door for others. Often, Satan wants to bring a gang of evil spirits into your life. Remember that the madman of Gadara had six thousand evil spirits in him.

Some years ago, thieves came to our house in the middle of the night. They ransacked the house and stole what they could from downstairs. In the morning, we were puzzled as we searched to find out how the gang had entered the house. Then we found a little gap in a window through which a small-sized person had entered. Once he got into the house, he opened up the rest of the house and let the rest of the gang in.

This is what Satan wants to do by tempting you repeatedly. He is searching for a door that he can pry open and let in other evil spirits. The demon of stealing opens the door for the demon of lying.

The sin of tempting God's servants is one of the most evil activities of demons. The devil was thrown out of heaven and has been tempting people ever since. Satan has inspired countless numbers of people to follow his example and tempt God's servants.

Many people are walking in the sins of Satan when they walk as tempters. Tempters deserve to be cast out and cast away forever. That is the only treatment a tempter deserves.

Watch out for those who do not respect you! Watch out for those who have come into your life to make you fall! Watch out for those who are there to test your resolve! Any person who comes into your life to tempt or test you is inspired by Satan. He is anointed from hell to destroy you.

Analyse every woman in your life and ministry. Ask yourself: is she a devil? Is she a literal demon sent to destroy your life and ministry? Does she respect the greatness of the call of God and the anointing on your life? Do not be led away by people who flaunt their delightful and appealing bodies on you. They are living devils sent from hell.

Analyse every man in your life today. Is he a living devil? Is he a person who is sent to tempt you? What does a devil do? A devil tempts, tests and seduces. Are you being tempted, tested and seduced by a person in your life?

Dealing with Tempters is Dealing with Satan

Then was Jesus led up of the Spirit into the wilderness to be tempted of the devil.

Matthew 4:1

When you deal with temptations and testings, you are dealing with Satan himself. When you allow tempters to run freely in your life, you are allowing the devil access to your life and ministry. It is a great mistake for you to allow someone to tempt you constantly. That person is a literal devil and must be removed from your life. Deal with the devil by dealing properly with your tempters!

CHAPTER 16

The Sins of a Devil: Tricks, Traps and Deception

And the great dragon was cast out, that old serpent, called THE DEVIL, AND SATAN, which DECEIVETH the whole world: he was cast out into the earth, and his angels were cast out with him.

Revelation 12:9

"One of you is a devil!"

How can you know when someone is a devil?

When somebody is a devil, he behaves exactly like the devil and deceives God's servants just as the devil did!

One of the most wicked sins of the devil is the sin of deception. The sin of lying to God's servants is one of the most destructive activities of demons. People get into the ministry and into certain jobs by deception.

Until you have encountered a trickster you may not know how dangerous deception can be. You may even get married because you are deceived. This will not happen to you!

A young man got married to a supposed virgin. He married this lady because he had the impression that she was a virgin. Some months after the honeymoon, he confided in me and said, "I always wondered if my wife was a virgin."

"Why?" I asked.

He said, "There was something strange about our first night together. It was just too easy."

He continued, "I had heard testimonies about how people struggled to have sex on their first night. In our case, there was very little struggle."

He went on, "Also, there were various things that she did to me that surprised me. I thought to myself, 'This is a very experienced person. She knows too many fantastic and amazing things to be a beginner'."

The brother was soon to discover that his wife was very far from being a virgin when he married her. Indeed, she had even been pregnant once before getting married. Wow!

The devil was thrown out of heaven because of his tricks, traps and deception. Satan has inspired countless numbers of people to follow his example and walk in the sin of deceiving men. People are walking in the sins of Satan when they walk in tricks and deception. A deceiver is a dangerous person to have around you. If you have a liar around you, you have a devil around you! Deceivers must be thrown out!

One of the great crimes of Satan was his attempt to deceive the Son of God. He tried to make Jesus fall into sin by deceiving Him with clever and difficult traps. Even up till today, scholars struggle to understand the temptation of Jesus Christ. The temptation of Jesus Christ was a cleverly disguised deception.

Again, the devil taketh him up into an exceeding high mountain, and saith unto him, ALL THESE THINGS WILL I GIVE THEE, IF THOU WILT FALL DOWN AND WORSHIP ME.

Then saith Jesus unto him, Get thee hence, Satan: for it is written, Thou shalt worship the Lord thy God, and him only shalt thou serve.

Matthew 4:8-10

Satan tried to turn the Son of God into a sinner. Satan wanted to trap Jesus Christ. Satan wanted Jesus to fall low so that He would not be able to stand upright before the Father in holiness. Watch out for those who will try to turn you into a sinner. That is Satan at work again to trick you.

Satan tried to deceive Jesus Christ. Watch out for those who try to deceive you.

Satan attempted to embarrass, disgrace and humiliate Jesus Christ by deceiving him. Through temptation, Satan attempted to cause the Son of God to fall. Watch out for those who try to deceive, embarrass, disgrace and humiliate you. Be careful of those who try to make you fall by deceiving you.

Satan wanted to trick Jesus Christ to be an ordinary person and not to be a holy person any more. Watch out for those who want to turn you into an ordinary person.

Any time you see someone trying to deceive, intimidate, harass and embarrass God's servant, you must discern the presence of Satan. You do not need a special word of knowledge to confirm this. This is exactly what Satan attempted to do to the Son of God. This is why he will be punished in eternal fire. Look at what happened to Ananias and Sapphira who tried to deceive Peter.

But a certain man named Ananias, with Sapphira his wife, sold a possession, And kept back part of the price, his wife also being privy to it, and brought a certain part, and laid it at the apostles' feet.

But Peter said, Ananias, WHY HATH SATAN FILLED THINE HEART to lie to the Holy Ghost, and to keep back part of the price of the land?

Acts 5:1-3

They were clearly filled with the spirit of Satan as they tried to deceive the man of God. Whenever you walk in deception, you are walking and working as a devil. Are there deceivers around you? If there are tricksters and deceivers around you, there are devils around you. You are delivered from every form of deception by the power of God!

CHAPTER 17

The Sins of a Devil: Accusing Men of God

And the great dragon was cast out, that old serpent, called the Devil, and Satan, which deceiveth the whole world: he was cast out into the earth, and his angels were cast out with him.

And I heard a loud voice saying in heaven, Now is come salvation, and strength, and the kingdom of our God, and the power of his Christ: for THE ACCUSER of our brethren is cast down, WHICH ACCUSED them before our God day and night.

Revelation 12:9-10

"O ne of you is a devil!"

How can you know when someone is a devil?

When somebody is a devil, he behaves exactly like the devil and becomes an accuser.

The Iron Man

I remember a vision I had. I was going in and out of a tall building. There were many people going in and out with me. Just outside the door of this important tall building, was a man sitting on the floor. He was slim and very strong and seemed to be made out of wires and steel. Every time I passed by, he said something about me that was not true. He would shout out and tell everyone that I was from a certain country and I was doing things that I had never done. Meanwhile, this man had never met me before! He did not know anything about me! I kept on telling him that I was not from that country and that I had never done any of the things he was talking about. But he kept on shouting to people that I was from that strange country and that I was up to no good.

At a point, I wondered if I was from that country and whether I had done all the things he was shouting about. The iron man, by his shouting, had drawn a lot of attention to me and was causing major problems for me. In the vision, I began to fight and struggle with this creature whose main aim was to announce wrong things about me and to say things about me that had no basis and were absolutely untrue. But this creature was very strong. He seemed to be made of flexible iron rods. I could not easily dislodge him from his position.

Then I heard a voice telling me to crush its head with a brick. I was being told to crush the demon with a much greater force. I needed to kill this creature because it was up to no good. That would be the only way to silence this terrible accusing creature that had planted itself at the door.

You see, that iron man was a demon. That is why he had super-human strength. He was up to no good. His work was to accuse me and create a thoroughly false and negative impression about me. His job was to weaken, unsettle and intimidate me by his accusations.

One of the most wicked sins of the devil is the sin of accusation. The sin of accusing God's servants is one of the most destructive activities of demons. Until you have encountered accusations, you will not know how disruptive, distracting and destructive accusations are.

The devil was thrown out of heaven because of this sin! Satan has inspired countless numbers of people to follow his example and walk in the sin of accusation. Many people are walking in the sins of Satan by continuing in the ministry of accusation. Such people are literal devils to you! Even if the accuser is an associate pastor, a journalist or a wife, that person is the devil to you! Such accusing people deserve to be disrespected, cast out and cast away forever. That is the only treatment an accuser and a devil deserve! That is how Satan was treated by heaven! He was thrown out!

When you deal with accusations, you are dealing with Satan himself. Satan is the master accuser. When you allow accusers to run freely in your life, you are allowing the devil to feel free in your ministry. It is a great mistake for you to allow someone to accuse you constantly. Deal with the devil by silencing accusers and accusations!

"Accuser of the brethren" is a title given to Satan. You must watch out for wives who accuse husbands continually. You must watch out for husbands who accuse wives continually! Such people have devils in them! Such people are living devils! It is important to understand how accusations work. Accusations are not levelled at people because they are evil. Accusations are levelled at people because the devil is at work!

We are accusable because we have all sinned and do continue to sin! If we say that we have no sin, we deceive ourselves and the truth is not in us! The presence of sin makes us easy targets for an accuser and that is why Satan loves to use his weapon of accusation. Watch out for the effects of accusation! Accusations result in division and confusion. When there are accusations, everyone suspects the other and no one is sure who is good and who is bad any more. This results in confusion and division. Because many accusations have some form of truth in them, no one is sure of what is true and what is a lie.

This is why a church, a family, a political party, a nation is utterly divided by the presence of an accuser. An accuser in a marriage destroys the happiness and unity between the couple. Couples that were deeply united grow apart and are forced to subsist together, because of continual accusations by one partner.

When a husband wrongly accuses his wife of having an affair with other men, she becomes confused and draws away from him. When a wife accuses her husband of having affairs with other women, he draws away from her. He becomes secretive in order to protect himself from his suspicious and accusative wife. The formerly happy and united family is then divided into different camps based on the accusations that have gone forth.

When Satan enters into a marriage, he may use one of the partners as a strong accuser. Make sure you are not employed or used by a dark angel to accuse your best friend. Accusations are the greatest deception ever thought of by the devil to destroy families and churches. Notice how Satan accused Joshua, the High Priest. Indeed, accusing and disgracing God's servants are Satan's main pastimes.

Then he showed me Joshua the high priest standing before the angel of the Lord, and SATAN STANDING AT HIS RIGHT HAND TO ACCUSE HIM.

And the Lord said to Satan, "The Lord rebuke you, Satan! Indeed, the Lord who has chosen Jerusalem rebuke you! Is this not a brand plucked from the fire?"

Now Joshua was clothed with filthy garments and standing before the angel. And he spoke and said to

those who were standing before him saying, remove the filthy garments from him." Again he said to him, "See, I have taken your iniquity away from you and will clothe you with festal robes."

Zechariah 3:1-4 (NASB)

Accusing, disgracing God's honoured servants is one of the common activities of Satan. In this classic scripture, we see Satan standing by God's servant, trying to take advantage of his filthy garments. Because we walk and live on this earth, our garments and lives are tainted by the flesh and its weaknesses. This same Joshua, who was being accused, was helping to rebuild the temple and Jerusalem.

Every single one of God's servants has the weaknesses of the flesh. Satan loves to point out the shortcomings and failures of those who love God. God is completely aware of our shortcomings and He chooses to use us in spite of our great deficiencies.

Watch out for anyone who constantly ridicules preachers. Watch out for anyone who accuses men of God of being dishonourable and sinful. Watch out for those who constantly question the motives of people when they are preaching. This is what Satan does!

Satan is an expert at questioning motives and suspecting good people of having ulterior motives for what they are doing. You will receive innumerable accusations as you serve the Lord. When a person is constantly accused, he lives in the presence of Satan and suffers unimaginable torment.

Accusation can destroy a Minister

The scripture tells us that Jesus Christ was crucified by the princes of this world. The actual translation of that scripture was that Jesus Christ was crucified by principalities. Remember that principalities are one of the types of evils spirits mentioned in the book of Ephesians.

Which none of the princes of this world knew: for had they known it, they would not have crucified the Lord of glory.

1 Corinthians 2:8

How did the principalities actually crucify Jesus Christ? They crucified Him through the Pharisees, the Scribes and the Jews who accused Jesus Christ and organised His execution. *The activities of the Pharisees were therefore the activities of devils.* Jesus Christ was crucified by the princes of this world. For a whole week before the crucifixion, the Lord was in the temple being questioned and examined (accused) by the Pharisees.

Then went the Pharisees, and took counsel how they might ENTANGLE HIM in his talk.

And they sent out unto him their disciples with the Herodians, saying, Master, we know that thou art true, and teachest the way of God in truth, neither carest thou for any man: for thou regardest not the person of men.

Tell us therefore, What thinkest thou? Is it lawful to give tribute unto Caesar, or not?

But Jesus perceived their WICKEDNESS, and said, Why TEMPT ye me, ye hypocrites?

Matthew 22:15-18

WE HEARD HIM SAY, I WILL DESTROY THIS TEMPLE THAT IS MADE WITH HANDS, and within three days I will build another made without hands.

Mark 14:58

The question I ask is, "Did these accusations have the desired effect?" The answer is, "Yes, they did. They worked."

The accusations, even though fantastic and contrary to the known character of the preacher, had the desired effect. Jesus was condemned to death on the basis of these accusations. Satan intends to bring an end to your ministry through baseless accusations. But God will deliver you from the power of the enemy and give you the ultimate victory.

Accusation is Intimidation, Provocation and Harassment

You must understand the spiritual and demonic nature of accusations, no matter how true they are. Satan is the accuser of the brethren. Demon spirits constantly accuse, intimidate and harass men of God. Do not consider the persistent accusations against your life as natural.

You must rise up in the spirit and deal with the powers and the creatures of the dark world that are behind the constant harassment and intimidation of your life and ministry.

Intimidation and harassment of ministers of the gospel is clearly demonic in nature. Ministers that are constantly accused often look harassed and unwell. If you are experienced, you will notice the harassment of these honourable servants on their faces.

Some ministers of the gospel are accused, intimidated and harassed by enemies, associate pastors, wives, journalists, and critics.

Today marks the end of the power of accusation in your ministry. Two weeks from now, you will see the end of your accuser. Your accusers will fade away just as the Pharisees faded away. He that hath clean hands will get stronger and stronger!

CHAPTER 18

The Sins of a Devil: Murder

Ye are of your father the devil, and the lusts of your father ye will do. HE WAS A MURDERER FROM THE BEGINNING, and abode not in the truth, because there is no truth in him. When he speaketh a lie, he speaketh of his own: for he is a liar, and the father of it.

John 8:44

Which none of the princes of this world knew: for had they known it, THEY WOULD NOT HAVE CRUCIFIED THE LORD of glory.

1 Corinthians 2:8

"**O**ne of you is a devil!"

How can you know when someone is a devil?

When somebody is a devil, he behaves exactly like the devil and kills people just as the devil did!

One of the greatest sins of Satan was to organise the murder of the Son of God. How could you kill the only begotten Son of God, the precious Lamb of God? What wickedness! What a cruel way to deal with the Saviour of the world! Watch out for those who hate Jesus Christ.

Watch out for those who hate Christianity and those who kill Christians.

It is the same thing that the princes of this world did to the Son of God. We are children of God. The princes of this world are organising people to fight Christianity. Satan is inspiring people to kill Christians all over the world. The same spirit of Lucifer that organised religious men called Pharisees to kill the Son of God, is organising religious men to kill and murder Christians in different parts of the world.

It is the spirit of Satan that hates Christ and Christians. What you see today is merely a continuation of the crucifixion of the Son of God. When Saul persecuted Christians and killed believers, Jesus appeared to him and asked him, "Why are you persecuting me?" When you kill Christians you are persecuting Jesus Christ Himself!

Men of religion have been used by Satan to kill, steal and destroy in the name of religion.

One of the most brutal sins of Satan is the sin of murder. The sin of murder is one of the most wicked activities of a devil. Until you have encountered the senseless murder of an innocent person, you may not understand how evil the sin of murder is. The devil was thrown out of heaven because he was a murderer. Satan has inspired countless numbers of people to become murderers. The devil directly inspires people to become killers. Wherever you see an increase in murder, armed robbery and terrorism, you are seeing an increase in satanic activity. Look at what happened to Job:

And the LORD said unto Satan, Behold, all that he hath is in thy power; only upon himself put not forth thine hand. So Satan went forth from the presence of the LORD.

And there was a day when his sons and his daughters were eating and drinking wine in their eldest brother's house:

And there came a messenger unto Job, and said, The oxen were plowing, and the asses feeding beside them:

And the Sabeans fell upon them, and TOOK THEM AWAY; yea, they have SLAIN THE SERVANTS with the edge of the sword; and I only am escaped alone to tell thee.

While he was yet speaking, there came also another, and said, The fire of God is fallen from heaven, and hath BURNED UP THE SHEEP, and the servants, and consumed them; and I only am escaped alone to tell thee.

While he was yet speaking, there came also another, and said, The Chaldeans made out three bands, and fell upon the camels, and have CARRIED THEM AWAY, yea, and slain the servants with the edge of the sword; and I only am escaped alone to tell thee.

While he was yet speaking, there came also another, and said, Thy sons and thy daughters were eating and drinking wine in their eldest brother's house:

And, behold, there came a great wind from the wilderness, and smote the four corners of THE HOUSE, AND IT FELL upon the young men, and they are dead; and I only am escaped alone to tell thee.

Job 1:12-19

The story above is a wonderful revelation of the satanic power behind robbery, killing, murder and destruction. As soon as Satan was released into the life of Job, several things happened physically. If you are spiritual, you will know that these events are caused by Satan and other demonic powers.

a. *Stealing and armed robbery:* Job's oxen and asses were stolen by the armed Sabeans.

b. *Murder:* Job's servants were killed

c. *A fire outbreak:* Job's servants and sheep were burned

d. *The destruction of his transport business:* Job's camels were stolen and the servants killed.

e. *The destruction of property:* Job's eldest son's house collapsed.

f. *Financial loss:* Job's businesses were destroyed.

g. *Family tragedy:* Job's children were killed.

All attacks on your life that involve stealing, killing and destruction are caused by the devil and his agents. Spending time to bind demonic powers and destroy their plans will protect you from such evil attacks.

Men who go around stealing, killing and destroying are walking in the image of Satan and are inspired by the devil himself.

Demon-possessed men have no pity and compassion on the people they harm. Their pitiless hearts reveal the presence of darkness and devils.

The thief cometh not, but for to STEAL, and to KILL, and to DESTROY: I am come that they might have life, and that they might have it more abundantly.

John 10:10

When you deal with thieves, murderers and destroyers you are dealing with Satan himself. When you allow thieves and destroyers to prosper around you, you are allowing demonic activity to flourish. It is a great mistake for you to open yourself up to thieves and murderers. Deal with the devil in your life by dealing properly with thieves, murderers and destroyers.

The devil comes to steal, to kill and to destroy but Jesus comes to give life. Can Satan affect the circumstances in your life? Indeed, he can. There is enough evidence in the Bible to show that Satan can and does influence circumstances in this life.

When Satan alters circumstances, it is to make them unfavourable, difficult and complicated for you. Most Christians do not realize that Satan is involved in manipulating situations and circumstances. Whenever there is a lot of stealing, killing and destroying you can be sure that demons are on the loose.

One day, I saw a spiritual monkey sitting on the burglar-proofing of my window. This was a big monkey, unable to pass through the small holes. I was startled because I realised the creature was trying to enter my room but had been blocked. When your eyes are opened, you will see many creatures attempting to do various kinds of evil against you. They exist in the realm of the spirit and are trying to get to you.

Satan sought permission to attack Job and created a series of circumstances and events which affected Job's life terribly. Each of the things that happened to Job was an occurrence in the natural, but orchestrated by Satan. If Satan could orchestrate them in the days of Job, then he can orchestrate similar events in today's world. No one should tell me that Satan has no part in the circumstances of life. Satan can manipulate circumstances in an evil way against your life. I want you to notice all the different things that Satan orchestrated. They are all events that look natural but are manipulated by demons.

1.   Satan caused the death of Job's children.

2. Satan organized the killing of Job's servants and workers. Satan is a murderer and the author of all forms of murder. Every nation that has a lot of murder has a strong presence of Satan.

3. Satan organized Sabean thieves to attack Job's business of oxen and asses.

4. Satan organized Chaldean thieves to attack Job's camel transport system. All the camels were stolen and Job was left without transport.

5. Satan caused a fire to burn down Job's business of sheep farming and to kill all the workers.

6. Satan orchestrated and initiated financial difficulties in Job's life by starting a fire that burnt down his business.

7. Satan arranged a great wind or storm to blow over Job's house. Satan tampered with nature and the weather in order to destroy Job.

8. Satan caused the collapse of Job's house. Satan physically attacked the home of God's servant, causing it to collapse.

9. Satan caused the deaths of Job's children in a freak accident when the house of his eldest son collapsed.

10. Satan orchestrated the funerals of many people in Job's life. His servants, his children and his loved ones died. Job had no choice than to organize multiple funerals.

11. Satan caused Job to develop a serious illness.

These chronic illnesses which do not kill but harass, intimidate, frighten and threaten the life of people are evil things organized by the devil. Sickness in general, is caused by the devil. But there is a type of circumstance in which the person is greatly intimidated by the presence of a threatening illness. It is not an easy thing to be under threat of death. This is why it is a terrible experience to be on death row, expecting to die at any moment.

Today, there are many people who labour under the foreboding threat of illness and death. This circumstance is caused by Satan. This is what Satan did to Job. Job did not die from the illness that Satan put on him. God was protecting him and he was actually shielded from death.

Burning Down a Night Club

Always remember that Satan can tamper with circumstances so that he can oppose you, frighten you and ultimately destroy you.

There was a pastor who struggled to minister in his own church. The atmosphere in the church was dead and anyone who preached there struggled to flow and to minister. Visiting ministers also struggled to flow and no one enjoyed ministering there.

The pastor of the church decided to wait on the Lord about the atmosphere in his church. On the seventh day of his fast, he was kneeling on the stage about three feet behind the pulpit. When he looked up, directly above the pulpit, the ceiling had disappeared. Sitting in the ceiling rafters, directly above the pulpit was a huge spirit that looked like a baboon.

He said to the creature, "You're going to have to come down." The spirit drew away as if he did not want to obey.

He shouted, "You, come down in the name of Jesus!" This creature fell down onto the pulpit and then jumped onto the floor.

The pastor then said to the evil spirit, "Get out of here." The creature said nothing but looked at the pastor as if to say, "I don't want to."

"Just march out of here in the name of Jesus," he said. The baboon marched down off the platform and the pastor marched right behind him. He would go four or five steps and stop and look at the pastor, almost begging. He would not move until the pastor said, "No, go on in the name of Jesus."

They continued to go down the aisle, stopping every four to five steps. Finally, the pastor went ahead of the spirit and held the doors open. Still, the spirit would not go until he said, "In the name of Jesus!" Eventually, the spirit reluctantly moved out of the door. He went down the church steps and got halfway into the churchyard. He stopped again and the pastor had to command him to continue on out of the premises.

"I command you to leave this premises and never come back again in the name of Jesus." The creature ran across the street and went about a quarter of a mile away from the church.

The pastor then described how he watched the spirit run into a nightclub. The next night, to his amazement, the nightclub burnt down. It is amazing how evil spirits can manipulate circumstances and cause fire and destruction. If you are a spiritual person, you need to understand the activity of evil spirits and constantly bind their power lest they take advantage of you or your circumstances.

This pastor later testified that the atmosphere in his church changed completely after that incident. Visiting ministers began to comment on how the atmosphere in his church was radically transformed.

It is important to pray and block all attacks of the enemy that come in the form of stealing, killing and destroying. Bind the works and activities of armed robbers in your life! Bind the works of stealing in your life! Curse the power of death, murder and destruction in your life!

From today, every power of wickedness against you is overturned! Armed robbers, thieves and murderers are blocked in Jesus' name! Every wicked being that looks at your home and plans to attack you goes blind in Jesus' name! Your enemies are blown away by the east wind. They will be found no more. Murderers and assassins are wiped out in the name of Jesus!

CHAPTER 19

The Sins of a Devil: Making Christians Fall

The Son of Man will send forth His angels, and they will gather out of His kingdom ALL STUMBLING BLOCKS, and those who commit lawlessness and will cast them INTO THE FURNACE OF FIRE; in that place there shall be weeping and gnashing of teeth.

Matthew 13:41-42 (NASB)

"One of you is a devil!"

How can you know when someone is a devil?

When somebody is a devil, he behaves exactly like the devil and becomes a stumbling block, making Christians fall just as the devil does!

One of the most devastating sins of Satan is the sin of making people fall. The sin of being a stumbling block is one of the most distressing activities of a devil. Until you have encountered someone who deliberately makes you fall down from where you were, you may not understand how evil the sin of being a stumbling block is.

The devil was dismissed because he was a destroyer. Satan has inspired countless numbers of people to follow his example of being a destroyer. The devil directly inspires people to be stumbling blocks to make other Christians fall. There are men and women who are sent into your life to bring you down. They are heavily inspired by the devil to walk in the same sins that Satan himself operates in.

The thief cometh not, but for to steal, and to kill, and to destroy: I am come that they might have life, and that they might have it more abundantly.

John 10:10

Satan has many evil plans for Christians and churches. He has devised many terrible snares and traps for men of God. If you look around, you will see the sad end of many great men of God. In one city I know of several pastors who ended up as homosexuals, fornicators, child molesters, criminals and prisoners. All these people were tricked and trapped by demonic devices and plans.

Lest Satan should get an advantage of us: for we are not ignorant of his devices.

2 Corinthians 2:11

It is important to recognize what extreme and wicked ideas Satan has for you just because you are serving God. Look at what he did to Job just because Job was a steadfast servant of God and you will have an idea of the kind of wicked devices Satan has for those who love the Lord.

When a man trains a boy in the use of his anus for sex, he has been inspired by Satan to destroy him and turn him into a homosexual. Remember that the devil is a specialist at destroying people's lives. When a man comes into a lady's life and trains her in sexual things so that she loses her purity, her innocence and her trusting heart, he has destroyed another virgin.

Watch out for people who make men of God fall into sin! They are agents of Satan and they are walking in the footsteps and patterns of Satan himself. Watch out for ladies who cause men to fall into sexual sin! They are sent by Satan to destroy the lives of young, pure men of God.

Hearken unto me now therefore, O ye children, and attend to the words of my mouth.

Let not thine heart decline to her ways, go not astray in her paths.

For she hath cast down many wounded: yea, many strong men have been slain by her.

Her house is the way to hell, going down to the chambers of death.

Proverbs 7:24-27

Beware of those who come around telling stories to discredit, blackmail and blacken the reputation of God's servant. Jesus warned and cursed all stumbling blocks who cause people to fall. "But whoever causes one of these little ones who believe in Me to stumble, it is better for him that a heavy millstone be hung around his neck, and that he be drowned in the depth of the sea" (Matthew 18:6, NASB).

A stumbling block causes a good person to trip and to fall to the ground unexpectedly and disgracefully. If you cause a fellow Christian or minister of the gospel to come down from his honoured place, you are a stumbling block. If you humiliate God's servant, causing him to fall, you are a stumbling block.

Don't forget the curse that Jesus has for stumbling blocks!

The Son of Man will send forth His angels, and they will gather out of His kingdom ALL STUMBLING BLOCKS, and those who commit lawlessness and will cast them INTO THE FURNACE OF FIRE; in that place there shall be weeping and gnashing of teeth.

Matthew 13:41-42 (NASB)

CHAPTER 20

The Sins of a Devil: Being a Serpent

Now THE SERPENT WAS MORE SUBTIL than any beast of the field which the Lord God had made. And he said unto the woman, Yea, hath God said, Ye shall not eat of every tree of the garden?

Genesis 3:1

"One of you is a devil!"

How can you know when someone is a devil?

When somebody is a devil, he behaves exactly like the devil and becomes serpentine in his nature, just like the devil! A serpent is a silent, non-communicative, poisonous creature. Watch out for people who do not communicate! Watch out for people who sit silently at meetings, never having anything to say or contribute!

One of the most distressing sins of Satan is the sin of becoming a secretive, deadly creature of camouflage, ambush and deadly traps. The sin of becoming a serpent is one of the dangerous moves of the devil. We all know that a serpent poses great danger to human life.

Until you have encountered the silent existence of a deadly snake like a black mamba, you may not understand how terrible it is for a snake to be around you.

The devil has been expelled from heaven because there is no place for snakes in heaven. Satan has inspired countless numbers of people to follow his example and become silent, secretive and non-communicative. Such people have many things in their minds but never speak!

The devil directly inspires people to become serpentine. Wherever you see an increase in silent, secretive, non-communicative men around you, be aware that a group of serpents are surrounding you.

Let us now see what Satan has done to us by coming to us in the form of a serpent.

1. Satan turned himself into a serpent to attack Adam and Eve.

Satan turned himself into a serpent so that he could launch deadly attacks on God's people. In the story of Adam and Eve, Satan is described as a serpent. Many people have wondered whether the devil was a literal serpent or a spiritual serpent. Human beings generally dislike snakes and it is most appropriate that Satan is called a serpent.

Whether Satan is a literal serpent or not, does not really matter. Once Satan is called a serpent, we must learn what it means for us to fight a serpent. Fighting the devil and overcoming him is literally the same as fighting a snake.

2.   **Satan turned himself into a serpent to set traps, lay ambush and surprise God's children.**

Now THE SERPENT WAS MORE SUBTIL than any beast of the field which the Lord God had made. And he said unto the woman, Yea, hath God said, Ye shall not eat of every tree of the garden?

Genesis 3:1

Fighting a serpent is to fight a creature that is a specialist of camouflage and ambush. Demonic surprises come from the very nature of the serpent. Many problems that come into our lives, come in the form of surprises. People's lives change because they are unable to recover from demonic surprises.

Demonic activities always include surprises. The surprise of an armed robbery, the surprise of sudden death, the surprise of a sudden illness, the surprise of a sudden change in the financial situation, the surprise of a change of government can destabilize a person for the rest of his life. Snakes are specialists of surprises and ambush!

People do not realise that many snakes actually live underground. This is why snakes mysteriously appear in houses and gardens to everyone's amazement. People ask, "How did this snake appear here?" I once saw a snake in my house! I could not imagine where it could possibly have come from. Snakes are secretive and they constantly come up with surprises.

To successfully deal with the serpent in your life, you must prepare yourself for possible surprises. You must think through and see what your response would be if you received a demonic surprise. It is only when you are prepared, that surprises do not have a devastating effect.

Surprise the devil by giving him a surprise for every surprise! Show him that you are ready at every turn and every corner. Be instant in season and out of season! Pray everyday and commit yourself to God. Show him that you were expecting him. Repel Satan in the name of Jesus and he will think twice about giving you such surprises.

3.   **Satan turned himself into a serpent to attack God's people in every area of life.**

Snakes are found everywhere and so are devils! There is no place on earth where snakes are not found. Even in the most decent and developed parts of the world, you will find snakes. Snakes are found in the forest, in the savannah, on the plains, in rivers, in the sea, in mountains, in snow and in dry parched deserts. Why is this? The Lord God said, "On your belly shall you go."

And the Lord God said unto the serpent, Because thou hast done this, thou art cursed above all cattle, and above every beast of the field; UPON THY BELLY SHALT THOU GO, and dust shalt thou eat all the days of thy life:

Genesis 3:14

Cursed to go on his belly, the serpent lost its legs and has been wriggling his way into every nook and cranny in this world. Snakes are the only wild animals found in civilised areas of the world. You will not find a lion in a suburban area but you will find a snake for sure. Fighting the serpent is a fight against a widespread presence of devils.

It is important for you to know that demon spirits are working against you in your home, in your marriage, in your business, in your relationships, in your car, in your computer, in your phone and in every conceivable way.

Demonic activity is found amongst the ushers, the choir, the administrators, the pastors, the associates, the security men, the singers, the businessmen and the drivers of your ministry. If your eyes could be opened, you would see them everywhere.

I once had a vision in which the Lord made me aware of the presence of devils all around me. I was lying in a room that had a lot of doors and windows. There were curtains and drapes hanging all around the room. In the vision, it occurred to me to look behind the curtains. Instead of going to the curtains, I sort of peeped under a curtain and to my utter amazement there was a thick snake lying at the foot of the curtain. The snake was not very visible because it was covered by the lowest part of the curtain.

Then I continued to look at the rest of the curtains. To my amazement, there were snakes lying at the base of all the curtains in the room. All the snakes were sleeping and all the snakes were thick, deadly, venomous creatures. I was terrified because I was in a room with many sleeping serpents. I always have goose bumps when I think of that vision.

Because devils can be found in every circumstance, it is important to be aware of their presence so that you protect yourself from them. You must bind them constantly and inhibit their activity in your life. You must create circumstances in which demons are unable to operate freely. You must speak against them because your words have power.

4. **Satan turned himself into a serpent to feed on the flesh of man.**

And the Lord God said unto the serpent, Because thou hast done this, thou art cursed above all cattle, and

**above every beast of the field; upon thy belly shalt thou
go, and DUST SHALT THOU EAT all the days of thy
life:...**

**In the sweat of thy face shalt thou eat bread, till thou
return unto the ground; for out of it wast thou taken:
FOR DUST THOU ART, and unto dust shalt thou
return.**

Genesis 3:14, 19

Cursed to eat the dust, the serpent has been feeding on dust,
including the flesh of human beings, which is also dust. Just
imagine a snake having a meal. As the snake pushes its prey
with its nose, it bites it, spits on it, it chews it and swallows
it. This process of the serpent feeding on the flesh (dust)
is what is harmful to Christians. As the serpent feeds on
the flesh (the dust), he provokes it, inflames it, stimulates it,
arouses it and poisons it.

Many people have their flesh demonically stirred up, aroused,
inflamed and stimulated. When the flesh is stimulated by
the feeding serpent, it develops unusual inflamed appetites
and abnormal desires. There are many people who have
unusual inflamed passions. They constantly need to have
sex with multiple partners. Some people also have abnormal
corrupted desires for sex; men burning with passion towards
other men and women burning with passion towards other
women.

These desires are demonically stirred up and created by
the presence of evil spirits. Many people have strong
uncontrollable desires and appetites for pornography and
masturbation. These abnormal appetites are the normal
desires that have been provoked, poisoned, aroused and
inflamed by the serpent "pressing his nose" into them.

It is important to recognise the power and activity of the
serpents that feed on our flesh. It is important to strike at
the root of these abnormal fleshly cravings. You must not
accept abnormal desires and passions as normal. You must

accept that they are abnormal! You must understand what is happening because the serpent is feeding on your flesh.

Resist the devil! Do not make a home for him by saying what is abnormal is normal!

How to Destroy the Serpent

It is very dangerous to cut off the tail of a snake or to hit it in the middle. This only stirs up a wild animal that begins to fight for its life. The way the serpent is killed is by striking it on the head. You must fight the devil in the right way! You must fight the devil with the name of Jesus, the blood of Jesus and the cross of Jesus Christ. These are the weapons you have been given to fight the devil. You cannot fight the devil with donations of oranges, tangerines and loaves of bread! You cannot fight the devil with your business ideas or your clever motivational speeches. The devil is destroyed by the blood of Jesus and the cross that secured your salvation.

Mysteriously, God has promised that the woman will give the winning blow against the serpent. Many solutions that men develop only make the problems worse. Men are trying to resolve the problem of drugs by legalising them. Wars have been fought to solve problems and to drive out tyrants. Many of these tyrants were only replaced with worse and more evil men. The reign of Hitler in Europe was replaced by the reign of Stalin and communism in Eastern Europe and Germany. Many are surprised when tyrants are replaced with more wicked and murderous leaders.

Things get more complicated as man tries to kill the snake in the wrong way. The seed of the woman, which is Jesus Christ, is the only solution that will destroy the serpent. Christ is the Way, the Truth and the Life! Christ in you is the hope of glory! This is why it is an insult to Christ when pastors become teachers of secular human solutions that have no power.

A pastor is someone who is sent to present Christ and the cross as the solution to all mankind's problems. It is a wonder that men of God would lay aside the preaching of the cross and champion human solutions.

If social work and non-governmental organisations were the solution to man's problems then why did Christ have to come and die on the cross? If the sinking of boreholes, the building of vocational schools, the building of orphanages, the building of toilets and the care of the blind, the deaf and the dumb were good enough to save humanity *then why did Jesus come to die for us on the cross?*

We are not saved by social work!

We are not saved by human kindness and human goodness!

It is important to strike the serpent on its head and not on its tail. Showing kindness, sharing food, having parties for the poor will not save people from their sins. Jesus died for our sins because there was no other way for us to be saved. Without the shedding of blood there is no forgiveness of sins!

Mysteriously and prophetically, women will cause the destruction of the devil. Today, women are feared greatly as the cause of many evils. They are seen to be the source of temptation and lust, causing men to fall into immorality, lasciviousness and adultery. However, the scriptures have predicted the opposite. Through the woman, a great victory will be wrought against the serpent.

God has declared that He will mysteriously use women to fight and destroy Satan. Because of this prophecy, it is important that you open yourself up to the role of women in your life and ministry. You must find a way to safely involve women in your fight against the enemy.

Your wife can be a key woman who will be used to help destroy your enemy. God will raise up other women who will play significant roles in your life to bring about the destruction of various enemies in your life.

Why Women Must Be Spiritual

This is why women must be particularly spiritual. Women must be spiritual if they are to ward off the satanic strikes and invasions of their lives by the devil. Several warnings from history show us that Satan intentionally targets women and introduces much evil to this world through women. Let us go through some of the well-known strikes that targeted women in the past.

Strike 1 against women: Satan's invasion of the human race targeted the woman. You will notice that the serpent did not speak to Adam at all. He completely ignored Adam in the garden and had personal discussions with Eve. Eve's own confession was, "The serpent beguiled me." This means that the serpent deceived, captivated, charmed and enchanted the woman. Satan was unable to do such things to the man so he did it to the woman.

Strike 2 against women: The invasion of this world by a group of fallen angels who had sex with women, was another strike that targeted women. Women were invaded through fornication. Giants and other evil creatures were the products of this evil attack.

Strike 3 against women: The destabilization of this world and the destruction of world peace is a satanic strike that came about through a woman. Through Sarah's influence and advice, Abraham gave birth to Isaac's challenger, Ishmael. Today, great tensions have been introduced into our world through the simmering conflict between Isaac and Ishmael.

Strike 4 against women: In the book of Revelation, you see how the dragon targets the woman because he knows that she will be the source of his destruction. A woman poses great danger to the devil for two reasons. The first reason is that she is prophetically and mysteriously the destroyer of the devil! The second reason why she is a danger to the devil is because she will give birth to men who can fight the devil!

And when the dragon saw that he was cast unto the earth, he persecuted the woman which brought forth the man child...

And the serpent cast out of his mouth water as a flood after the woman, that he might cause her to be carried away of the flood.

Revelation 12:13, 15

CHAPTER 21

The Sins of a Devil: Occupying and Possessing Humans

Then was brought unto him ONE POSSESSED with a devil, blind, and dumb: and he healed him, insomuch that the blind and dumb both spake and saw.

Matthew 12:22

And they that saw it told them how it befell to HIM THAT WAS POSSESSED with the devil, and also concerning the swine.

Mark 5:16

And at even, when the sun did set, they brought unto him all that were diseased, and THEM THAT WERE POSSESSED with devils.

Mark 1:32

"One of you is a devil!"

How can you know when someone is a devil?

When somebody is a devil, he behaves exactly like the devil and enters churches, families and nations just as the devil does and destroys them from within!

One of the most unfortunate sins of Satan is the sin of entering human beings, occupying them and living in them. It is a crime to enter homes where you are not welcome! It is also a crime to enter a house and destroy everything there. It is a crime to enter a home and kill, hurt and afflict the owners of the homes. In the three separate scriptures above, you can see how Satan entered and possessed a man and also possessed several human beings. This is the greatest crime of wickedness ever done by the devil against the human race.

Until you have encountered a demon-possessed person, you may not understand how evil the sin of entering, occupying and living in human beings is.

Satan has now inspired many people to follow his example and enter churches and homes secretly to destroy them. The devil directly inspires people to join the leadership of a church and destabilize it.

Usually, expelling only one person from the church leadership, will end the confusion, the division and the unhappiness in a church. This is because that person is a planting of the devil and is walking in the sins of Satan to destroy the church from within.

How Satan Occupies Humans

Amazingly, human beings have received a slow but sure impartation of demonic nature. There are several steps that have taken place over the years, that have caused humans to share in the sins of Satan. Human beings have gradually taken up the nature of Satan as devils have sought after them, oppressed them, possessed them and imparted their nature to man. Let us go through the stages that have led to this great wickedness in human beings.

1. DEVILS SEEK OUT HUMAN BEINGS TO DESTROY THEM.

Be sober, be vigilant; because your adversary the devil, as a roaring lion, walketh about, SEEKING WHOM HE MAY DEVOUR:

1 Peter 5:8

Without knowing it, you are the devil's mission. He is looking for you and he is looking to destroy you and end your life. God's power is coming alive in your life and you are being set free from all forms of ambush and entrapments.

The devil has decided to behave like a lion. His only dream is to devour you and to devour me. Think about that! Should we not equally spend time finding him and sprinkling the blood of Jesus on him? It is time to rise up and rule in the midst of your enemies. It is a contest of power and you must display the greater power over and against the power of the enemy. Power against power! It is time to destroy the lion that spends his time hunting you down.

The Lord said unto my Lord, Sit thou at my right hand, until I make thine enemies thy footstool.

The Lord shall send the rod of thy strength out of Zion: RULE THOU IN THE MIDST OF THINE ENEMIES.

Thy people shall be willing in the day of thy power, in the beauties of holiness from the womb of the morning: thou hast the dew of thy youth.

Psalm 110:1-3

2. DEVILS OPPRESS HUMAN BEINGS.

How God anointed Jesus of Nazareth with the Holy Ghost and with power: who went about doing good,

and healing all that were OPPRESSED OF THE DEVIL; for God was with him.

Acts 10:38

Many people are oppressed by devils. Many of the afflictions of human beings are caused by devils. Almost every sickness and disease is caused by devils. A disease is "not being at ease". Whatever causes your "not being at ease" is a disease.

It may be a financial disease, a physical disease or even a marital disease. The devils are hard at work to oppress God's creation. They are truly wicked spirits with no good intentions for the human race.

As devils oppress human beings, the human beings become weaker and more vulnerable. As human beings weaken in their resistance to devils, they eventually become fully possessed.

3. **DEVILS POSSESS HUMAN BEINGS.**

And they come to Jesus, and see him that was POSSESSED WITH THE DEVIL, and had the legion, sitting, and clothed, and in his right mind: and they were afraid.

Mark 5:15

Whenever a devil possesses a human being, he takes over and does what he pleases with the human being. The result is usually the greatest kind of suffering, humiliation and death.

The mad man of Gadara, who was stripped naked, living in the cemetery, cutting himself with stones, is a good example of someone who was fully possessed by the power of the devil.

When the devil possesses a person, the person lives a life that makes no sense. All his actions stand against good reason. When the devil possesses a person, he acts like the devil himself.

When the devil possesses a person, he becomes a living, moving, physical devil. Jesus spoke of Judas Iscariot and called him a living, moving, physical devil. Jesus said, "Have not I chosen you twelve, and one of you is a devil?" (John 6:70). Before Judas turned into a devil, Satan entered into him.

Notice the scripture below. After Satan entered into Judas, he became a living devil.

THEN ENTERED SATAN INTO JUDAS surnamed Iscariot, being of the number of the twelve.

Luke 22:3

Jesus answered them, Have not I chosen you twelve and, ONE OF YOU IS A DEVIL?

John 6:70

4.   **DEVILS IMPART THEIR NATURE OF WICKEDNESS TO HUMAN BEINGS.**

When the unclean spirit is gone out of a man, he walketh through dry places, seeking rest, and findeth none. Then he saith, I WILL RETURN INTO MY HOUSE from whence I came out; and when he is come, he findeth it empty, swept, and garnished.

Then goeth he, and taketh with himself seven other SPIRITS MORE WICKED than himself, and they enter in and dwell there: and the last state of that man is worse than the first. Even so shall it be also unto this wicked generation.

Matthew 12:43-45

Many devils have occupied human beings and consider human beings as a home. Tenants are known to destroy buildings and impart their nature and culture to the building. This is why landlords do not rent their houses to certain people. Landlords object to certain people from certain nations and cultures occupying their houses. I have heard landlords declaring that they would never rent their houses to certain people from certain countries.

This is also why landlords receive a deposit before the tenant can enter the house. This deposit is used to repair the damages the tenant will 'impart' to the house.

Jesus taught us how the devil that goes out comes back with seven other 'tenant devils'. By crowding into human beings, these devils definitely impart something to the human beings.

Anyone who lives in a house imparts something to the house he lives in. If he is a scruffy person, he imparts the scruffiness to the house. If he is a melancholic person, he imparts tidiness to the house. These wicked spirits come and find the house tidy, swept and garnished. With wicked demons present, the house is gradually destroyed.

Wicked spirits have imparted their wickedness to their human hosts! There has been a gradual mixing of the nature of wicked spirits with the nature of human beings. Human beings have gradually become as wicked as devils!

Unfortunately, the human race is contaminated and is being made to commit the exact same sins that Lucifer committed.

5. **DEVILS TEMPT HUMAN BEINGS TO FALL INTO THE SAME SINS SO THEY RECEIVE THE EXACT SAME CONDEMNATION.**

Then was Jesus led up of the Spirit into the wilderness to be tempted of the devil.

Matthew 4:1

The devil wants human beings to commit the same sins that he did so that they will be condemned with the same condemnation of Satan.

Satan's goal is to tempt and test human beings who claim to be serving God! Many things you experience are simply tests. Many of them are set up by devils who seek to destroy you by making you fall. You will not fall in Jesus' name! Satan seeks to bring you down to his level.

Satan accuses you even when he does not have a factual basis for his accusation. Can you imagine how he will condemn you when he has a real basis for accusing you? Satan is seeking to bring you down to his level so that you will be condemned with the same condemnation of the devil.

Not a novice, lest being lifted up with pride he fall into THE CONDEMNATION OF THE DEVIL.

1 Timothy 3:6

Satan wants you to do what he did so that you will be as guilty as he is. When you commit the same mistakes that the devil did, you will be as guilty as he is. When you are guilty, Satan will have a legal reason to request your presence in hell with him.

You must therefore be aware that every one of the sins of Satan is being offered to you today on a silver platter. Many Christians walk in the sins of Satan and fall into the condemnation that the devil has. The devil is truly condemned, but you are not! If you joke with this revelation, you may one day walk in the sins of Satan and experience his condemnation.

I know many people who have behaved exactly like the devil and brought into their churches the same confusion, division and commotion that Lucifer brought into heaven.

Do you want to be 'the devil' and 'the Satan' of your home and your church? It is time for you to gain understanding into the sins of Satan in Jesus' name! By the grace of God, you will never walk in those sins!

CHAPTER 22

The Punishment of a Devil

And the devil that deceived them was CAST INTO THE LAKE OF FIRE AND BRIMSTONE, where the beast and the false prophet are, and shall be tormented day and night for ever and ever.

Revelation 20:10

"**O**ne of you is a devil"!

So what is the punishment that Satan will receive for his many sins of separatism, division, murder, tempting Christians, attempting to humiliate Christ, starting wars and killing people? What will be the punishment of a person who behaves like the devil?

When somebody behaves like the devil, he receives exactly the same kind of punishment that the devil did. You can watch these kinds of people closely, and you will see that the end of them is the same: isolation, darkness, demotion and destruction.

It is important to know how to handle people who behave like the devil. Failure to handle them properly will cause their powers to increase and their destructive tendencies to multiply. There are many pastors who have associates and assistants with satanic traits. It is important to relate appropriately with pastors who exhibit satanic traits.

One of the ancient scripts tells us that if Lucifer had not been cast out of heaven none of the angels would have survived his deception, politicking and separatism. Indeed, you must learn to punish satanic behaviour appropriately.

Instead of outright dismissal, you find some ignorant pastors rather promoting people who are rebellious and have separatist tendencies. I want you to study each of these punishments that God meted out to Satan and his fallen angels so that you will know how to properly deal with rebellion in your life and ministry.

When people become rebellious, they must not be given access to the church that they have rebelled against. Unfortunately, people open up the doors of the church to rebellious people, thinking they are walking in love. Opening your doors to the devil is not walking in love! It is walking in foolishness! When you allow rebellious people into the pulpit or even into the church premises, you are making a mistake. No one is wiser than God. If God dealt with rebellion and separatism by casting it down, you must do the same!

There are many interim punishments that have been meted out to the devil and demons. Their final punishment however, will be implemented in the end.

Let us now look at the different punishments that Satan and his fallen angels are going to have to endure because of the many things they have done. This is how you must punish rebellious people in your world. You must deal with them in exactly the same way that God dealt with Lucifer.

How to Punish Disloyal People

1. Punish them with outright dismissal.

And prevailed not; neither was their place found any more in heaven. And THE GREAT DRAGON WAS CAST OUT, that old serpent, called the Devil, and Satan, which deceiveth the whole world: he was cast out into the earth, and his angels were cast out with him.

Revelation 12:8-9

Satan was sacked! Satan was thrown out of his position as a senior angel. Satan was dismissed. He was not prayed for! He was not counselled! He was not advised! He was not rehabilitated! He was cast out!

That is the only treatment for disloyal and rebellious separatists. It is only when you are inexperienced that you will try counselling and praying for people who are filled with the spirit of separatism and independence.

2. Punish them by denying them access.

And prevailed not; NEITHER WAS THEIR PLACE FOUND ANY MORE IN HEAVEN.
And the great dragon was cast out, that old serpent, called the Devil, and Satan, which deceiveth the whole world: he

was cast out into the earth, and his angels were cast out with him.

Revelation 12:8-9

Satan was denied access to heaven. Satan's place in heaven was taken up. It was very important for Satan to be prevented from coming back to heaven. When anyone is sacked from a job, the keys to the office will be taken from them and they will no more be able to come in and out like they did when they were employed there.

There are pastors who leave churches but are welcomed back and allowed to come to the compound and even pose as returning heroes. Some people even come with peace offerings for the pastor they rebelled against. When you allow these people to come around, you are making a mistake of glorifying rebellion. You are allowing separatists to inspire others to rebel.

I remember a pastor who rebelled and separated himself from the congregation. After some months, he attended a conference of my pastors. When I saw him, I asked that he be ushered outside. His presence was undesirable and unacceptable. I did not want his presence to give the wrong message. I loved him and I still do, but I would not allow him to inspire rebellion among the faithful ones.

His presence at the conference was unacceptable to me and I found it completely unbiblical to include him in that meeting. Read your Bible carefully and do not be childish when it comes to dealing with rebellious people. *Neither was their place found in heaven any more.* And neither should any rebellious person's place be found in the church they rebelled from any more.

3.   Satan is punished with confinement.

And the great dragon was cast out, that old serpent, called the Devil, and Satan, which deceiveth the whole world: he was cast out INTO THE EARTH, and his angels were cast out with him.

Revelation 12:9

Satan was confined to the earth as part of his punishment. His activities are now limited to the earthen realm. People who follow the sins of the devil are forced to live in darkness and difficulty for the rest of their lives. Absalom was forced to live in exile because he had rebelled against his father. The earth is a difficult place for rebels to live.

It is a place which has been cursed. The earth is a place of sweating and struggling. Satan and all evil spirits were confined to the earth and its atmosphere. They are forced to roam around from place to place, seeking rest. Apparently, there is no good resting place on earth for these evils spirits. That is why they earnestly try to enter human beings. When they enter human beings they see the light and enjoy rest. "When the unclean spirit is gone out of a man, he walketh through dry places, seeking rest, and findeth none" (Matthew 12:43).

Devils are able to express themselves by feeding on human beings and causing intolerable hardship to human beings. In this world of confinement, demons are forced to feed on the flesh of human beings and that in turn causes intolerable abnormalities and variations to human life.

Just as mosquitoes suffer and perish from hunger when they do not have blood to drink, evil spirits struggle when they do not have human life to feed on. The confinement of demons to the earth is a terrible experience of restlessness.

4.   **Punish rebellious people by keeping them in darkness.**

And the angels which kept not their first estate, but left their own habitation, he hath reserved in everlasting chains UNDER DARKNESS unto the judgment of the great day.

Jude 1:6

In our world today, there is an invisible dimension in which bacteria, virus and parasites live. These creatures are not visible to the naked eye, but exist and cause much harm to human beings. Many of the viruses are so small that it takes a microscope as big as a house to view them. The fact that you cannot see this invisible dimension does not mean that it does not exist.

Understanding the realm in which bacteria and viruses live will help you to understand the realm of darkness. It is a realm where there are things you cannot see. They are real and they affect everything that is going on in the world that you can see.

Satan has been confined to a realm of darkness within the earth's atmosphere. Apparently, there is a realm in our world called "darkness". In this realm, everything is dark, scary, spooky and evil. One kind of demon power is called "rulers of the darkness of this world".

Rebellious people must be kept in darkness. They must not be allowed to see the light that faithful people enjoy. I once had a pastor who rebelled painfully against me. He separated himself and inspired other pastors to do the same. Remember, separatism is Satanic in its origin.

One day, I received a call from this separatist. He wanted me to ordain him in his church. I refused to ordain him. I wondered why I should go to a rebellious separatist and glorify him with an ordination service. Why would I want to lay hands on somebody who despised me? Why should I empower a separatist by laying hands on him and praying over him? I don't find God ordaining the devil or consecrating him as a bishop after he separated himself from the other angels in heaven!

Indeed, I refused to ordain him. Rebellious people must remain in the darkness which they have chosen for themselves. This is how God dealt with Satan, the separatist, who caused much confusion and conflict in heaven. This pastor had also caused much confusion and conflict in my church. He had sparked many years of conflict that had never existed before in our ministry. Such people must be dealt with in the same way that God dealt with Satan – darkness!

5. Punish them by restricting them.

Demons and evil spirits are restricted. This is an important part of the punishment of demons. They do not know everything, they do not see everything and they cannot go everywhere. You must always remember that demons are beings that are in chains.

This is why changing location can actually take you out of the influence and power of certain evil spirits. There are people who fall to sin as soon as they change location. There are others who jump back to spirituality when they change their location. These restricted demons are unable to follow you wherever you go. Evil spirits are restricted in more than one way.

Demons do not understand everything you say or decide. Praying in tongues is one of the most powerful weapons because it keeps your prayers, plans and pursuits out of range from demons. There are evil spirits that come around to hear you talk and plan important things. This is why certain attacks begin when you begin to plan certain things.

Separatists must be restricted. They must not be allowed to have every privilege that faithful ones are given. If you allow them to come to your house and into your life, you have not understood what you are dealing with.

I once had a rebellious separatist pastor who was perfect in his ways until iniquity was found in him. The iniquity I am speaking of is the iniquity of separatism and evil independence.

This separatist pastor departed from our church and set up his own independent ministry nearby. He then travelled to a certain country and requested a bishop whom he did not know to become his spiritual father. There are lots of rebellious people out there who are seeking endorsement from anyone who would do so.

After many years of silence, this man called me up on the phone and said he had a surprise request to make. I wondered what surprise he was talking about. Then he said, "I will be getting married and I would like you to officiate the ceremony." I was amazed that this fellow would ask me to officiate and bless his wedding. Why did he not stay faithfully under my leadership if he thought I had such power to bless a wedding?

How could someone he no longer respected have any power to bless his wedding? Why would he not call on his new spiritual father to perform these duties for him? To cut a long story short, I told him that I would not be able to bless his wedding. You see, rebellious separatists must be restricted and not granted the same access and freedoms they had before.

But this fellow would not take no for an answer. He asked that I send some other senior bishops to bless his wedding! I was amazed that someone who had stepped away and caused a virtual war in our church would even think of asking for such a favour.

Was he expecting us to come, glorify and endorse his activities? I had the difficult task of informing him that there was no such person who could come and bless his wedding. It is important to deal with separatists by restricting them in the same way that God has restricted Satan, the original separatist!

And the angels which kept not their first estate, but left their own habitation, he hath reserved in EVERLASTING CHAINS under darkness unto the judgment of the great day.

Jude 1:6

6. Accept that the people you love have changed in their very nature.

And the great DRAGON was cast out, that old SERPENT, called the Devil, and Satan, which deceiveth the whole world: he was cast out into the earth, and his angels were cast out with him.

Revelation 12:9

Satan has become an ugly serpent and dragon. His nature changed once and for all when he fell from heaven. When human beings fell from grace, they also changed in their nature. In *"The First Book of Adam and Eve[1]"*, we learn how the nature of Adam and Eve was changed dramatically when they fell from grace. When they were in the garden, they were filled with the grace of a bright nature and had hearts not turned towards earthly things.

After the fall, Adam said to Eve, *"[2]Look at your eyes and at mine which before beheld angels praising in heaven without ceasing. Now we do not see as we did; our eyes have become of flesh. They cannot see like they saw before.[2]"*

Adam said again to Eve, *"[3]What is our body today compared to what it was when we lived in the garden.[3]"*

Adam and Eve were appalled at the changes that had taken place in their bodies. Everything was different. The punishment for falling into the temptation was grievous. The punishment affected their very appearance.

You will notice that when people walk in sin their very appearance changes. You can virtually see evil on people's countenance if you are perspicacious.

Satan experienced a terrible degeneration and change in appearance when he fell from grace. He was completely metamorphosed into an ugly, fallen and limited creature. Remember that Satan was known for his beauty, brightness and attractiveness. Today, he is known for his ugliness and frightening appearance.

Today, there is nothing more revolting than a serpent. Human beings cringe when they see a serpent. A lizard is a kind of dragon and is equally disgusting to see or touch. Instead of being perfect in beauty, bright and attractive, Satan is now an ugly disfigured serpent and dragon.

You must keep yourself from falling into Satan's dark deceptions and temptations. They cause a change in your very appearance.

7.   **Accept that the devil will be tormented.**

And, behold, they cried out, saying, what have we to do
with thee, Jesus, thou Son of God? Art thou come hither
TO TORMENT US BEFORE THE TIME?"

Matthew 8:29

Demons are going to be tortured and tormented forever.
Torture and torment are what happens to the worst of prisoners.

Satan and his hordes are fully aware of this terrible time of
torture that is soon to be upon them. They fear it and they dread
it. When Jesus came to this earth, they thought He had come to
start the season of torment before the set time.

8.   **Satan will be punished to swim in the lake of fire
forever.**

Then shall he say also unto them on the left hand, Depart
from me, ye cursed, into everlasting FIRE, PREPARED
FOR THE DEVIL AND HIS ANGELS:

Matthew 25:41

Why is Satan Not in Hell Right Now?

Why does it seem that some rebellious people prosper? Why
is it that some separatists seem to flourish even though they have
done so much evil?

Indeed, we all wonder why these evil spirits have not been
sent to hell instead of being allowed to roam around on earth.

Satan and other fallen angels have committed great crimes
against God and against human beings. They have destroyed the
entire human race, corrupted the world and brought much evil to
God's creation.

When Jesus came to this earth it was quite clear that evil
spirits were freely roaming around, inhabiting human beings,

causing diseases and doing evil. On one occasion, as many as six thousand evil spirits were found in one human being! Why weren't these evil beings sent to hell long ago? When Jesus cast them out, they resisted Him and said, "We want to go into the pigs."

On one occasion, the evil spirits told Jesus that it was not the time for them to be punished. "Why have you come to torment us before the time?" they asked.

And when he was come to the other side into the country of the Gergesenes, there met him two possessed with devils, coming out of the tombs, exceeding fierce, so that no man might pass by that way.

And, behold, they cried out, saying, what have we to do with thee, Jesus, thou Son of God? ART THOU COME HITHER TO TORMENT US BEFORE THE TIME?

Matthew 8:28-29

There are individuals who are neither desirable nor helpful but must be part of the society until their final punishment is meted out to them.

Have you never seen people who are accused of terrible crimes who are free to go until the final verdict is passed? Michael Jackson was accused of various crimes, but was allowed to go home every day until the judgment day. If he had been found guilty, he would have been taken into custody and kept in prison for many years.

President Charles Taylor of Liberia was accused of crimes against humanity. Before the final verdict on his case was passed, he was allowed to live a semi-normal life in a nice European prison. He was allowed to receive visitors, interact with people and make phone calls. He even fathered a child during this season! I am sure he watched the news and read the newspapers every day.

These freedoms were only granted him because the final verdict had not been reached. Until his final judgment, he lived a semi-normal but restricted life in the Hague. After the final judgment was passed, his circumstances changed and he was led away into a more difficult and permanent place of imprisonment without freedoms.

This is the exact same fate that Satan, the fallen angels and other evil spirits are facing. They are in a restricted and darkened state, able to do certain things in their weakened condition. Today, evil spirits influence lives, cause havoc, deception, murder and destruction, even though they operate in a dark and restricted world.

However, a day is coming when the final verdict will be passed over them. After that, their imprisonment will be absolute and they will be cut off, unable to influence the world any longer.

Whenever evil spirits saw Jesus they recognised their future judge. This is why they screamed out, "Have you come to torment us before the time?" The evil spirits were frightened! They thought the judgment day had come.

The final judgment of Satan and his angels is to swim in the lake of fire; burning and drowning for eternity. This punishment is the final penalty that Satan, fallen angels, princes of this world, principalities, powers, thrones, wicked spirits, unclean devils and demons will have to pay for all that they have done to this world and to the human race.

Satan will be gasping, drowning, burning and screaming as he swims through the flames in the lake of fire. ⁷⁷May all the enemies of God perish in the same way!

References

Chapter 10

1. Lumpkin, Joseph, B. (2010) *The Encyclopedia of Lost and Rejected Scriptures: The Pseudepigrapha and Apocrypha* 1 ed. Blountsville, Ala.: Fifth Estate.

2-2. Ibid.

Chapter 13

Excerpts from:

"What is Secularism?" *www.gotquestions.org.* Web. 20 Jan 2017. Retrieved from https://www.gotquestions.org/what-is-secularism.html

"List_of Wars_of Independence" *en.wikipedia.org.* Web. 20 Jan 2017. Retrieved from https://en.wikipedia.org/wiki/List_of_wars_of_independence

Chapter 22

1. Lumpkin, J. (2010) *The Encyclopedia of Lost and Rejected Scriptures: The Pseudepigrapha and Apocrypha* 1 ed. Blountsville, Ala.: Fifth Estate.

2-2. Ibid.,Chapter IV:8-9

3-3. Ibid., Chapter IV:10